Tolkien's *Mythology for England*
A Middle-Earth Companion

Edmund Wainwright

Anglo-Saxon Books

Published 2004 by
Anglo-Saxon Books
Frithgarth
Thetford Forest Park
Hockwold-cum-Wilton
Norfolk England

British Library Cataloguing-in-Publication Data. A catalogue record for this book is available from the British Library.

ISBN 1–898281–36-X

They are proud and wilful, but they are true-hearted, generous in thought and deed; bold but not cruel; wise but unlearned, writing no books but singing many songs, after the manner of the children of Men before the Dark Years. .... It was in forgotten years long ago that Eorl the Young brought them out of the North ...

J.R.R. Tolkien, *Lord of the Rings: The Two Towers*

Introduction

This book is about the historical and mythical dimension to Tolkien's Middle-Earth, and the many ways in which a knowledge, at once both deep and broad, of the history of the English language led J.R.R.Tolkien to create a mythic world in which to explore many of the themes he felt to be important in life.

The Lord of the Rings has been a story of phenomenal popularity and success in the second half of the 20th century and now looks set to continue into the 21st with the release of Peter Jackson's three blockbuster films based on the books. A West End musical is also at the planning stage.

Tolkien's other writings, including the children's book *The Hobbit* and the epic mythical narrative *The Silmarillion*, have remained in print ever since they were first published. Even his scholarly writings (such as *Beowulf: The Monsters and the Critics*) and his small-scale tales (such as *Farmer Giles of Ham*) have been cherished by fans of his greater works – fans who would not normally have given them a second glance without the association to the name of Tolkien.

The Matter of Middle-Earth

A school of literary criticism has built up around what Professor Tolkien himself might have called *The Matter of Middle-Earth*. Books by esteemed authors have argued back and forth about the meaning and the detail of the tales, in terms which indicate that the subject is taken every bit as seriously as mediaeval history or textual studies. A lively debate has raged in cyberspace about many aspects of the story and the intentions behind it. All this activity exists despite that fact that the book does not deal with anything having objective reality: none of it is *true* in the real world, and never has been!

How then can one explain this astonishing phenomenon? Why do level-headed people care so passionately about the doings of folk in a world which does not exist? Why do so many of us read the books through, then immediately go back to the beginning and re-read the entire story a second or even a third time? How did *The Lord of the Rings* come to take on many of the qualities of a cult or even a religion? And what, above all, gives *The Lord of the Rings* its unique flavour, which sets it apart from the rest of the fantasy genre?

To state what may be obvious, *The Lord of the Rings* is a work different in kind from all others. It offers the reader a unique experience: a visit to an otherworld every bit as engaging as our own; a world challenged by serious issues of right and wrong, of justice, of the responsible use of power. How was a bookish, reclusive scholar able to confront these issues and turn them into a masterly narrative of love, death, honour and duty? The answer to this question lies in the personality and life-experiences of the man himself.

Any appreciation of the work must begin from an assessment of three critical factors: Tolkien's personal life and experiences; his professional life and studies; his religious beliefs.

In this book, Chapter 1 *The Master of Middle-Earth* offers a brief overview of Tolkien's life, career and achievements. Some assessment of the influence of his deeply-held Catholic beliefs is also made there.

In Chapter 2 *A Mythology in the Making* we will look at the uses of myth in literature and some themes, ancient and modern, which are helpful in understanding Tolkien's work.

Certain thematic elements are developed in Chapter 3, *The Legacy of Heorot*[1], which offers a series of parallels between the literature of Tolkien's professional study – a body of work which he deeply loved and admired for itself – and the corresponding motifs in his sub-created world of Middle-Earth, with regard to Anglo-Saxon historical and legendary themes, as well as to other cultures with which he was familiar.

Chapter 4 deals at some length with the languages and scripts of Middle-Earth, and their relationship to the ancient languages which Tolkien studied professionally.

In Chapters 5 and 6 there is an examination of the popularity and appeal of the books within the English-speaking world, and outside it.

Finally, an outline timeline is provided to help the reader tie up contemporaneous events in the story.

The aim of this book is to offer a key to help the reader understand where Tolkien's sources lie, with a view to encouraging others to explore the literary landscapes he knew so well.

A Note on Conventions

OE here means "Old English", the language of the English in the Anglo-Saxon and early mediaeval periods. **ON** means "Old Norse", the Scandinavian language of the same period.

An asterisk (*) before a word means that it is nowhere recorded but is reconstructed by scientific principles.

---

[1] The book *The Legacy of Heorot* by Larry Niven is a futuristic retelling of the *Beowulf* story, dealing with nature's revenge on humankind through a super-metabolic animal predator. While Tolkien would probably have disapproved of the mode of the tale (science fantasy) he would certainly have approved the sentiment. He also might well have applauded another writer's attempt to adapt something from Northern myth into a work of creative fiction. *Heorot* was the name of the hall of King Hrothgar of the Danes, which Beowulf cleansed of its supernatural predators.

1. The Master of Middle-Earth

John Ronald Reuel Tolkien was born at Bloemfontein, South Africa in 1892 to English expatriate parents Mabel and Arthur Tolkien, a clerical officer in a bank. Arthur Tolkien had emigrated to the colony to further his career.

The family name, Tolkien, is unusual: it is in origin a German name and an ancestor of his may have come to England from Saxony in the previous century. The two elements Tol + kien correspond to the English words 'dull' and 'keen', and imply 'foolishly brave' or 'reckless'. Nevertheless Arthur Tolkien was thoroughly English, and his wife's family, the Suffields, had deep roots in the West Midlands.

His experiences in Africa played little part in the later life and writings of John Tolkien, although it is recorded that he was once terrified by a huge spider – an ordeal he was later to use to good literary effect.

Tolkien's father died in 1896, and his mother returned to England, taking up a leased house at Sarehole, near Birmingham. John and his brother Hilary spent their childhood years in what was then a quiet, rural village under the shadow of its flourmill. The area was dominated economically and politically by the massive engineering and industrial plants in Birmingham, then one of the leading mass-production centres of the western world. The sense of the sooty-black madness of industrialised society creeping into the heart of the countryside runs through all of *The Lord of the Rings* and was a theme taken up in many of his other writings (*On Fairy Stories* is its most explicit statement). Tolkien felt very deeply the sense of loss accompanying the spread of the industrial zone, and it is fair to say that he hated what this process was doing to both people and places.

The family moved to King's Heath, a suburb of Birmingham, where the grounds of the Tolkiens' family house were adjacent to a railway line. Birmingham's industrial might rested on the city's access to cheap fuel: coal, mainly from South Wales. John Tolkien later recalled seeing the endless procession of coal-trucks passing down the track bearing romantic and unpronounceable names such as Senghenydd and Nantyglo. The youngster's imagination was fired by the possibilities implied by this: both the linguistic curiosity, and the notion of a road at the doorstep leading off into the unknown.

In 1900 Mabel Tolkien and her sister May Suffield broke with the religious tradition of the family and converted to Roman Catholicism. Neither the Tolkiens nor the Suffields apparently approved of this conversion, and contact between them all but ceased. John and Hilary were henceforth to be raised as Catholics under the guidance of the local priest, Father Francis Morgan. Mabel Tolkien was diagnosed with the then-incurable condition of diabetes in 1904, and died in October of that year. The two boys were fostered out to an aunt, and later took lodgings locally with a Mrs. Faulkner. Father Morgan, who was half-Spanish, half-Welsh, eventually took the two brothers in and helped to develop John's already promising flair for languages. Having mastered both Greek and Latin, John was beginning to explore many other languages of Europe both ancient (such as Gothic) and modern (such as Finnish). He had also begun to investigate the creative possibilities of devising his own languages.

John had formed a friendship with Edith Bratt, an orphan and fellow lodger in the Faulkner household. When, at the age of sixteen, John's feelings for the nineteen-year-old Edith were evidently becoming more serious, Father Morgan forbade further contact between them until John reached twenty-one.

With his gift for languages and his voracious appetite for 'philology' (the study of languages, nowadays called 'linguistics') John went off to Exeter College, Oxford, in 1911 to study the Classics, the Germanic languages – especially Old English and Gothic - and also Welsh and Finnish. Failing to achieve the highest grades in the Classics course, his attention switched to the study of linguistics with particular attention to the languages of the ancient northern European world, where he felt considerably more at home. In 1913 he resumed his relations with Edith but he still had a long way to go down the road to a successful career before he could consider developing the relationship.

As part of his study of Old English literature, John Tolkien had to be familiar with all the major works in that language. Understanding the texts is not always as easy as it appears, despite the obvious linguistic continuity within the language over the last 1500 years. There are two main reasons for this: first, due to the disruption caused by the Norman invasion, in which the native culture of the English was suppressed for two centuries, a certain amount of what was written in Old English refers to concepts that we no longer understand. Second, at the Reformation, with the breaking and destruction of monastic libraries, a vast amount of Old English literature was destroyed, the manuscripts torn up and recycled for industrial purposes. These factors in combination mean that many Old English texts contain words which are unique – they just do not survive in any other texts. Sometimes their meaning is evident; sometimes it can be deduced by searching the vocabularies of other Germanic languages for 'cognate' or related forms; in some cases, the meaning is entirely lost. It has taken the skill, patience and scholarship of many generations to reconstruct these broken fragments of the past, and to tease out the meaning of these ghost-words. Tolkien set himself to the study of the problems associated with this branch of research, drawing on his wide knowledge of ancient languages and his skill in identifying the ways in which languages have developed through time.

The turning point in his creative life came during study of the Old English poem now called *Christ*, one of a handful known to have been composed by the poet Cynewulf. The poem contains the phrase:

Eálá Earendel engla beorhtast ofer middangeard monnum sended

Lo! Earendel - of angels brightest over middle-earth - to men sent.

or in more usual English "hail Earendel, the brightest of angels sent to men on earth". Despite the reference to the 'angel', the name *Earendel* is not biblical, but an ancient (pre-Christian) English name for the morning-star, Venus. Speculating on the cultural world of the man who could combine two things he cared about so passionately – ancient lore and Christian commitment – Tolkien began using the mysteries of the ancient texts to fuel the creation of imaginary realms where the two met, collided and combined.

In 1913 Tolkien took a temporary job as tutor in Dinard, France; the experience left him with a considerable distaste for the French. On his return to England, Edith converted to Catholicism and their relationship began to deepen. However, the outbreak of war in 1914 put immediate plans on hold, yet the young Tolkien devoted his energies to achieving his first class degree in 1915. He accepted a commission in the Lancashire Fusiliers in 1916, and prior to leaving for France he and Edith married.

He saw action on the Western Front in the Somme offensive. All but one of his close friends from childhood had been killed; John Tolkien escaped that fate in the insane carnage of the trenches when he contracted 'trench fever' – a form of typhoid – which saw him invalided out to a long convalescence in a Birmingham hospital, followed by a recuperative stay with Edith in Staffordshire. During his time in the trenches, Tolkien was deeply moved by the comradeship he found among the other ranks. These men, mostly lowly agricultural workers from rural districts of England, performed daily acts of outstanding heroism in support of each other yet they were never accorded official recognition. He saw the butchery of war close-up, in the most inhuman of all modern conflicts, and above all he saw how these men were able to overcome the most appalling conditions of filth and misery with good humour and courage. The experience could hardly fail to affect his outlook on both warfare and the meaning of commitment to loved ones.

During the war, he had engaged his creative powers with work on a narrative of a sea-rover, Earendel, whose journeyings led him so far out into the encircling waters that he became a star in the heavens. His linguistic powers were absorbed in the creation of a language based loosely on Finnish, which he called Quenya. The writings of this period formed the basis of the tales later assembled into *The Silmarilion*; they were subsequently edited for publication under the title *The Book of Lost Tales*.

His health never recovered to the point where he could resume active service, but he nevertheless saw out the war on the home front and rose to the rank of lieutenant. While stationed at Hull, Edith and John took a walk in the nearby woods at Roos. In a woodland clearing, Edith danced for him – an event which moved him greatly. He was later to use this theme in the tales of Beren and Lucien (with whom he identified himself and his wife) and later Aragorn and Arwen.

The love of the English countryside comes through everywhere in his writings: of gently rolling hills and thick woodland interspersed with glades of wild flowers, of homely inns serving good food and good beer, of straightforward folk going about their business and trusting others to do the same.

Post-war, Tolkien took employment on the *Oxford English Dictionary*, and he allowed some of his creative writing to receive its first public airing. Among the circle of bookish friends at Oxford, his work and his ideas met a favourable reception and he was encouraged enough to continue developing his themes. In 1920 he was appointed as Reader in English Language at the University of Leeds, where he collaborated with E.V. Gordon on an edition of the classic mediaeval poem *Sir Gawain and the Green Knight*. He and Gordon set up the "Viking Club" of which the main activities were reading the saga literature of Iceland, and drinking beer. Work on Elvish languages and forgotten myths continued in this stimulating atmosphere, but in 1925 Tolkien successfully applied for the Rawlinson and Bosworth Professorship in Anglo-Saxon back at Oxford University.

His time at Oxford was spent in the teaching of his subject (the history of the English language), and in researching the background to it. He did not publish many academic papers, but some of his contributions to scholarly debate marked a turning-point in the discussion. Most notable in this context is the essay *Beowulf: The Monsters and the Critics*, in which he decried the then-prevalent study of the *Beowulf* poem as a source of historical information: he believed that the poem had been composed in the first place as a work of creative fiction, and should be treated in those terms. In other words, instead of trying to tease out history from legend, we should read the work first for enjoyment of it as poetry. In the light of the creative work Tolkien was engaged in himself, it seems likely that this paper shows his mind was turning towards preparing the tales of the Elves for public airing.

Due to his close familiarity with Anglo-Saxon and mediaeval texts, Tolkien knew that England had once possessed a complex local mythology every bit as rich as that of Ireland or Greece. It is *almost* forgotten, and largely beyond recall. Not far from his room in Oxford, on the Berkshire Downs, stand two evocative monuments within a couple of miles of each other. The Uffington White Horse is a chalk-cut hill figure of unknown antiquity; it depicts a running quadruped, possibly a horse or some mythical beast. On the Ridgeway track to the east there stands a Neolithic burial mound, known as *Wayland's Smithy* since Anglo-Saxon times. Wayland (Welund) was the English smith-god whose artefacts were held to be of miraculous strength and power. The place and the name remain, but the knowledge of Welund has melted away; local folklore is too fragmentary and too garbled to help.

The Norman invasion had destroyed the cultural continuity on which recapturing myth from folk-belief and local traditions must rely, and the Reformation had deprived us of the written materials needed to recreate it from its recorded elements. England's native mythology was gone, replaced by the interesting but alien Arthurian myths, which themselves went through a long process of re-writing to end up as the threadbare and listless collection of tales we have today. Accepting that recapturing accurately the myths of ancient England would be impossible, Tolkien decided that an alternative could be devised. If we could not have Welund back, we could replace him with someone similar enough to be a useful substitute. The feeling for place and theme which can be glimpsed in the few surviving scraps of tradition from Anglo-Saxon times convinced him that there was enough to work with. All he needed to do was to use the pattern of the ancient tales to weave a new cloth – a mythology for England.

Tolkien played no active part in the Second World War, being already past forty at its outbreak, although it is recorded that from early on he despised the German National Socialist movement for the ignorant and insensitive way in which it distorted the 'northern spirit' he loved so much. Although, as a university professor, he must have been an establishment figure, there is a clear thread of anti-authoritarian feeling in *The Lord of the Rings*, where the lust for power and control is the fatal flaw in many characters, and is portrayed as the weakness which the One Ring can exploit. Having seen what modern-day dictatorship could do to normal, decent human beings, there is no doubt that he felt that the corrupting tendency of power was always a poison in men's hearts.

In 1945, Tolkien exchanged his professorship for the equivalent at Merton College where he remained until professional retirement in 1959. He and Edith had four children: John, Michael, Christopher and Priscilla. Christopher, a university lecturer, undertook the posthumous publication of many of his father's works. Outside his academic occupation, Tolkien was involved in what we would now call a literary studies and creative writing group known as The Inklings. Another member of this group was C.S. Lewis, who wrote the *Narnia* fantasy stories including *The Lion, the Witch and the Wardrobe*. The two scholars shared a deep religious conviction and a love of fantasy writing.

Bedtime stories for his children allowed him the opportunity to try out narrative ideas on an audience without preconceptions; some of these tales have also been published since his death (*Roverandom, Mr. Bliss*). The crucial point came, according to his own account, during a grindingly dull session of essay-marking in which one student had obligingly left a blank page. Tolkien casually jotted down the sentence "In a hole in the ground there lived a hobbit" and then decided to find out what a 'hobbit' was and why it should live in a hole. Expanding the theme, he made up a children's tale of a dragon and a lost treasure, and the journey of a group of adventurers to recover it. The story enjoyed some popularity among the Oxford children, and was typed up for circulation; a typescript came into the hands of an employee of the publishing firm George Allen and Unwin, and the professor was commissioned to complete the tale. In 1937 it was published under the title *The Hobbit* and has never been out of print since, so successful was it.

Public demand for more tales of the hobbits and their adventures encouraged the publishers to request further material. Tolkien had only the grandiose and expansive work-in-progress *Quenta Silmarillion* which was not meant for a readership of older children as *The Hobbit* had been. Although admitting the high literary quality of the narrative, the publishers felt that there was no commercial market for such a work. Going back to the drawing board, Tolkien began work on “the New Hobbit” in close consultation with Rayner Unwin of George Allen and Unwin. Rayner Unwin believed in the literary worth of the project and agreed to underwrite the estimated one thousand pound loss which publication would entail. Publication of the three volumes in 1954-5 took place under the title *The Lord of the Rings.*

The public reaction was overwhelming. The critics either loved the work or loathed it. Many of the more influential voices in English literature ranged themselves firmly against the books; to their dismay, sales proceeded from strength to strength. The BBC broadcast an abridged version for radio in 1956 and popularity swelled further. In the dark days living under the threat of nuclear extinction, or waiting for the trudge of Soviet boots across Western Europe, the courage and fortitude of ‘little people’ were an important source of comfort and inspiration.

Commercial success was pushed to a new level in 1965, however, in an unforeseeable way. A pirate version of the book was published in the USA in paperback format, making it affordable to many students caught up in the drug-fuelled counter-culture of American universities at that time. The ensuing legal action over the book brought it to the public’s attention, ensuring commercial success in that market. Professor Tolkien became rather wealthy on the proceeds, and was flattered by the strong positive feelings his work evoked in his worldwide readership. With success came unwanted celebrity, and it became necessary for him and Edith to move house, retiring to Bournemouth.

Edith died in 1971, whereupon John Tolkien returned to Oxford, to rooms in Merton College. He died in 1973. He and Edith are buried together in Wolvercote cemetery, in a single grave. The headstone gives their Elvish names: *Luthien* and *Beren.*

2. A Mythology in the Making

Tolkien's express purpose in his creative works was to create a "mythology for England". That statement poses two questions: "What is a mythology?" and "Why did England need one?"

Myth, Legend and Folklore

Mythology is ancient, deep-rooted and universal. All human societies have myths, which deal with the eternal challenges and questions of human existence – love, death, man's place in the cosmos, the nature of life, free will, fate. Psychologists such as Sigmund Freud and, especially, Carl Jung were able to analyse dreams in their (modern day) patients using themes from ancient mythic narratives – we have all heard of the Oedipus Complex, in which the male child tries to win the affection of his mother and exclude his father, named after a character in Greek myth.

A 'mythology' is the complete set of myths of a particular 'cycle'. We speak of Irish mythology or Greek mythology and by these terms we mean the ancient tales of the Irish and the Greeks concerning their gods, their exploits and their dealings with mankind. Myths are almost always explanatory, they open up and clarify matters, the way things are in the world. They also accompany ritual – a rite is an enactment of divine myth on earth. Often myths explain the unknown, and so impose order on the chaotic universe around us – they account for observable facts (for example, they explain why the sun and moon pass overhead, why the seasons cause changes in the weather, why society is structured in a particular way). Myths explain social customs, and give them meaning and purpose – they are especially sacred in nature, and the enactment of myth through ritual is a way of affirming membership of a specific group.

All these things are associated with myth in ancient societies, but myth is still with us and much modern creative work is mythic in intent and effect.

Myths are distinct from legends, which are the doings of great men and heroes in the past, usually in the geographical region where the legends are told. They often account for place-names and geographical features; they deal with specific persons and places in the past. Legends shade into folklore, which is a complex system of tales and customs associated with specific peoples.

Mythology has as its main purpose the ordering of history within a cosmic framework – making the deeds of (real or imagined) persons significant and meaningful. This framework demonstrates that the cultural group (tribe, chiefdom or nation) using the myths are in some way special. Myths often deal with the creation of the world, the ordering of the passage of time and the moral and social codes in place on earth. They regulate the relationship of men and gods or other beings.

A mythology is, then, a powerful ordering principle in the right hands, with elements of religion and social patterning. I do not think Tolkien was offering Middle-Earth as a plan for social change in mid-20th century England. Rather he was attempting to sub-create a possible set of mythic narratives which might resemble, in their general thrust and character, those which existed among the ancient English. The crucial words here are 'might resemble' – Tolkien never claimed that the stories were actually those known to the ancient English, nor that anything in them was genuine lore of the ancient north. His book was true to the *spirit* of northern myth and legend but made no attempt to be true to the *letter* of it – in fact, he avoided this process, which would have been deliberately misleading. In the preface to *The Lord of the Rings* he describes the book as if it were a genuine ancient document which he translated from 'Westron', the Common Speech of Middle Earth. He substituted English for Westron, and represented more ancient and conservative forms of the language in the text with more ancient and conservative forms of English - a convenient fiction which avoided many pitfalls in handling ancient Germanic languages and figures from myth.

Myth is a deep-seated need in communities. Wherever groups of human beings gather, they cannot help devising rites – from simple protocols (every bar, pub and office has its list of "do's and don't's") to complex initiation ceremonies (many professions have annual meetings at which a new intake of youngsters joins the group). These behaviours are sanctioned by myths.

A concrete example: the cricket event known as "The Ashes" is played annually between England and Australia. It commemorates a crushing defeat of the English team by the Australians more than a century ago, after which *The Times* published an "obituary" (*see below*).

Ever since then, the match against Australia has been fought for "The Ashes", a symbolic prize – English pride in the national game. What is important here is not the historical event, but the rite of the annual contest. The "Ashes" have assumed a mythic dimension quite independent of their true origins in an ultimately meaningless sporting fixture.

In Affectionate Remembrance

of

E N G L I S H C R I C K E T,

which died at the Oval

on

29th A U G U S T, 1882,

Deeply lamented by a large circle of sorrowing friends and acquaintances

R.I.P.

N.B. - The body will be cremated and the ashes taken to Australia.

Myths in Literature

All those who have read *The Lord of the Rings* appreciatively have been struck by the powerful sense of connectedness in the story. Unlike any other work of modern fantasy fiction, *The Lord of the Rings* feels like a genuine tale set in a genuine (though past) world in which millennia of history are embedded in the background detail, the wisdom and lore of the protagonists. This is no accident. Tolkien the creative writer was able to collaborate with Tolkien the linguist and Tolkien the mediaevalist to produce a unique and consistent effect. With a deep and wide-ranging knowledge of the tales of the ancient past at his fingertips, Tolkien was perfectly placed to draw on the mythic traditions of Europe, some of which may date from as far back as the Neolithic period some five millennia ago.

In his greater works – *The Lord of the Rings* and *The Silmarillion* – he rescued myth from the backwaters of literature and restored it to its rightful place at centre-stage. In so doing, he created a new literary genre – vastly different from standard works of fantasy – which can only be truly understood if the reader has some background knowledge of mythology. The casual reader may enjoy Tolkien's work as a wide-ranging tale of adventure and courage, but the reader who wishes to understand why *The Lord of the Rings* has such a profound effect on him must make the effort to understand the sources on which Tolkien drew.

The narratives of *The Lord of the Rings* and *The Silmarillion* are presented as works of mythology, complete in themselves. In *The Lord of the Rings* we are also able to enjoy the mythical narratives of the various peoples of Middle-Earth, as they conceive of them. This double-layering of myth in the tale accounts for some of the richness in the story. Nevertheless, Tolkien did not simply lift themes and devices from a fund of mythic literature and drop them into his text at random. As a student of the greatest English literature and a gifted wordsmith, he was able to use his knowledge creatively: to weave the threads of ancient myth into a wholly new cloth. He was able to balance the traditional themes with a good deal of personal invention, so that one-for-one correspondences between Tolkien's characters and figures in genuine mythology are rare.

Tolkien's first creative work – *Earendel* – was an attempt to use ancient material in a new way. It is based loosely on the Norse myth known as Þórr and Aurvandil's Toe, where the god Þórr (Thor) offers to carry a dwarf named Aurvandil across an icy river. He places the passenger in a basket over his back, but the dwarf's big toe sticks out and becomes frozen hard. Þórr snaps off the toe and hurls it into the night sky where it becomes a star. (This is a typical example of myth being used to explain the world: the name of the star is Aurvandil's Toe, and the myth shows how this came to be.) The story is known from a medieval manuscript, but must be ancient. We know this because the name Aurvandil is the Norse equivalent of the Old English name Earendil found once in an Anglo-Saxon document. It occurs also in German as Orentil. The reference may be to the morning star (Venus).

The Heroic Model

A whole body of investigative study has been devoted to examining the elements that are typical for the 'hero' of myth: across a great many cultures, languages and religions there is a surprising similarity in the stories associated with certain 'great men' of the past. Lord Raglan proposed a checklist of attributes of the 'hero story' of which the following is a summary:

1. The hero's mother is a royal virgin, and
2. his father is the king and
3. a relative of the hero's mother.
4. The conception is unusual and
5. the hero is believed to be the son of a god.
6. There is an attempt to kill him at birth but
7. he is rescued and removed and
8. he is reared anonymously far away.
9. His childhood is unrecorded but
10. when he reaches manhood he returns to his kingdom (or goes to his future kingdom).
11. He fights and defeats a powerful adversary and then
12. marries a princess (usually the daughter of his adversary) whereupon
13. he becomes king.
14. His reign is untroubled at first and
15. he regulates conduct through laws but
16. eventually he loses favour and
17. is stripped of power and driven out whereupon
18. he dies in mysterious circumstances
19. on top of an elevated place.
20. Any children he has do not succeed him and
21. his body is not buried in the normal manner, but
22. he has a holy memorial.

This series of events in the typical hero's story – to which the lives of such diverse characters as Arthur, Perseus and Moses conform - can be matched against the story of Aragorn in *The Lord of the Rings.* His mother, Gilraen, was a descendant of the royal line of Arnor while his father was Chieftain of the Dúnedain and so also a member of the Arnor royal line (points 1, 2, 3). Arathorn and Gilraen were married due to a prophecy by his maternal grandmother (point 4). Aragorn was adopted by Elrond (not a god, but chief among the Elves) and brought up in Rivendell under the name Estel in order to protect him from attack as Isildur's heir (points 5, 6, 7, 8). There is nothing to tell of his childhood until he learnt of his heritage, fell in love with Elrond's daughter Arwen and left his childhood home to serve in the armies of Gondor (points 9, 10). During the War of the Ring he revealed himself to the enemy, Sauron, with his sword, Narsil, and was a major player in the forces assembled to overthrow Sauron (point 11). He was crowned King Elessar of Gondor and soon after married Arwen (points 12, 13). His peace was proclaimed at the end of the War of the Ring and he reigned uneventfully for many years (points 14, 15). Eventually, he died of his own volition on a hilltop in Minas Tirith (points 18, 19) and lay unburied for a while (point 21). As a twist to the tale, it was the widowed Arwen who went to the forest of Lothlorien, where she died alone (*contra* point 17); her son by Aragorn, Eldarion, succeeded him (*contra* point 20).

There are points of contact in Aragorn's tale with many legendary heroes and sovereigns, beyond the generalised Raglan scheme above. Among these would be the king's healing powers, and the support and advice of a venerable spiritual guide (Gandalf, the Merlin of Aragorn's story). The thrones of turfs on which Aragorn, Eomer and Imrahil are seated before his coronation replicate the traditional seat of King Conchobar in the Ulster cycle of myth. This is Tolkien the mediaevalist at work, using material he knows well to make a new garment out of old cloth.

Perhaps the most telling thing in Aragorn's story is not the way in which it follows the normal model, but rather the ways in which it does not. Points 16 and 17 are absent: Aragorn does not betray the promise of his youth, he fulfils it and is loved by his people till the end.

Sudden Reversal

One theme from myth which Tolkien managed to use to good effect in his books is what he termed *eucatastrophe* in *On Fairy Stories*. A catastrophe is properly a sudden turn in the tide of events which leads to disaster. Myth employs this device regularly, but also the converse – *eucatastrophe* – in which an unlooked for and sudden reversal brings the overthrow of evil and the triumph of good. Catastrophe is the defining characteristic of Greek tragedy, while eucatastrophe likewise defines the tales of Faerie. It has become a hackneyed theme in modern literature and film – the sudden arrival of the 7th cavalry to save the waggon train, the one-in-a-million shot that lays the villain low, snatching victory from the jaws of defeat – but in the right atmosphere and circumstances it can be very moving. Tolkien described it as "joy beyond the walls of the world, poignant as grief" and indeed many readers have been moved to tears by the last glorious ride of Theoden of the Mark, or the unexpected overthrow of the mighty Nazgûl, who fears nothing from men, by a halfling and a mortal woman. This 'joy beyond the walls of the world' is moving because the situation does not deny the possibility of failure; instead it faces failure squarely, and refuses to flinch.

Linked to this notion of 'reversal' in the course of the story is the idea of 'fate'. In writing a 'pre-Christian' narrative Tolkien could not introduce Judaeo-Christian ideas of fate and punishment which would sit ill with the essentially northern European tradition he was trying to sub-create. He could, however, bring in what the Anglo-Saxons called *wyrd* which can be roughly translated as 'the course of events' or 'what happens'. *Wyrd* is not a fixed, pre-ordained series of actions and outcomes; rather, it is a tendency or predisposition in history. *Wyrd oft nereð unfægne eorl ðonne his ellen deah* says the *Beowulf* poet: 'Wyrd often spares a man who is not doomed while his courage holds'. In Norse tradition, a personification of 'fate' is found in the Three Weird[1] Sisters, the *Nornir* (Norns) who weave the skein of men's lives; no such explicit idea is brought into the narrative. Indeed, Tolkien never really states that any event in *The Lord of the Rings* is pre-ordained, yet there is a very definite sense of unseen powers at work: Gandalf remarks that he senses that Gollum, Bilbo and Frodo were *meant* to bear the Ring, but not by its maker. Frodo has prophetic dreams during his stay at Rivendell, and on looking into Galadriel's mirror sees what was, what is and what may be – but Galadriel does not claim that what the mirror shows must inevitably come to pass. Boromir also dreamt that he should look for the Sword that was Broken, and his dream brought him to Rivendell in time for the Council of Elrond. Even the dour, unimaginative Sam Gamgee, believing Frodo dead, realises that he was meant to take up the quest of the Ring. The existence of prophecies implies that some foreknowledge of events must have been gained in the past, but this theme is never really developed beyond statements of proverbial truth, such as 'oft evil will shall evil mar'. There is, above all, the sense that all the characters have free will, and that the contending forces of good and evil will adjust their strategies according to the choices the key figures make.

Immortality and Escape from Death

Another mythic theme which Tolkien successfully adapted to his design in *The Lord of the Rings* is that of 'immortality' - or more properly 'deathlessness', since his Elves do not die through old age but can nonetheless lose their lives to illness and war. For some European societies the afterlife was a continuation of life on earth; this is evidenced in the Norse traditions of *Valhöll* (Valhalla) and the Everlasting Battle in which warriors slain on the battlefield are revived by magic. An afterlife of earthly type but in another place may also have formed the basic idea behind the ship-burials, such as the famous example from Sutton Hoo in East Anglia. The royal ship was loaded with treasure which may have been intended to cross to the otherworld with its owner.

Tolkien explicitly identified deathlessness with the Elves and constructed a society for them around the notion that a long-lived people would have every opportunity to perfect all their arts and crafts.

---

[1] 'The weird' sisters of Shakespeare recall the three *Nornir*, and remind us that *weird* is the modern English form of the word *wyrd*.

The apparent death and subsequent recovery of heroes is a central theme in many traditions: in fact, in one definition, a hero is 'twice-born', having been taken beyond the veil of death and returned to the mortal world. Tolkien uses this theme in two ways in *The Lord of the Rings*: often characters are believed to be dead but miraculously survive, or are healed; in the case of Gandalf, the character has apparently physically died and then been returned to Middle-Earth to complete his task. (Who returned him, and how, is not dealt with in the book, but in *The Silmarillion* Tolkien was more explicit.)

Nevertheless, Tolkien the committed Catholic could not resist the urge to hint in the tale of Arwen and Elessar that there might be a re-union with loved ones in some form of life after death.

Time-shift

Allied to the deathlessness of the Elves is the peculiar way in which they are able to manipulate time. This power is inherent in the three Rings of Power which the leaders of the folk (Elrond and Galadriel) received. With these rings they create areas over which they have complete control, like pockets of Elvenhome on Middle-Earth. In these regions, time flows at a different rate from the normal time of the world.

The basis for this manipulation of time lies in the many folk-tales concerning the Elves, whereby time goes by at a different pace in their realm. Usually a visitor is persuaded to enter Faerie, often through an open burial mound or other portal. There are two variants: either the visitor stays one night in the mound and on his return finds that a hundred years has past above ground, or he spends a long time with his hosts and on his return finds that no time has passed at all. In some versions, he is warned that he can never return, but he wearies of the life of revelry and as soon as he steps back into the real world he becomes a pile of dust.

Tolkien wove a very exact chronology into his tales, and in *The Lord of the Rings* the narrative often mentions the date or the phase of the moon. This rigorous use of timescales adds to the air of authenticity in the tale. The out-of-time events then acquire much greater significance through being mysterious. As with languages and customs, Tolkien used different calendars for the various races and groups.

Men calculate time using a solar year of twelve months (i.e. much as we do). Elves also use a solar calendar, but divided into six seasons based on the life-cycle of plants; being deathless, the Elvish long-year is 144 solar years. The hobbits' calendar has intercalary days (i.e. days which come between months, and do not belong to either). This parallels the Anglo-Saxon practice of inserting a midsummer festival called *Liða* (the hobbits' *Lithe*) between June and July, and another called *Geol* (Yule) at midwinter between December and January. The solstices and equinoxes feature in the books as important turning points, and this feature mirrors the ancient belief that these quarter days were pivotal, points of transition.

Descent into the Dark

A relatively common theme in myth involves the hero confronting his fears, alone, in a dark underground chamber or tunnel; this is the mythic counterpart of the resolution of problems through dreams. Tolkien used it several times in *The Hobbit* to develop the character of Bilbo Baggins from a relatively useless travelling companion to the status of valued comrade and 'burglar'. In *The Lord of the Rings* the mood is darker, the menace greater. Examples are the barrows, Moria, the Glittering Caves in the hill behind Helm's Deep, the Paths of the Dead and Shelob's Lair. The hero normally emerges with something of value – either a physical object, or some knowledge which will assist him in his mission. Emerging from the descent, he appears to have reached a turning point in his quest from which there is no return to his previous life.

Aragorn in particular enacts the descent several times in the tale, most notably when he rides the Paths of the Dead and emerges with the ghostly army at his back.

An example from Anglo-Saxon tradition is Beowulf's descent into the mere to grapple with Grendel's Mother; the whole episode has a dream-like quality which may betray its mythic origin.

War in Heaven

Elements of the *Rings* narrative are very reminiscent of the tale of the War in Heaven, in which two groups of gods enlist mortal heroes to wage a destructive war of annihilation. The forces line up and the first encounter is often indecisive. The leader of the gods' opponents is captured and imprisoned, but later breaks free in time for a second fight. The conflict culminates in a climactic battle which is so vast and so fierce that the whole Earth is ravaged with fire. From this final conflict a new order emerges, replacing the previous powers with a fresh world characterised by abundance, harmony and rebirth.

This tale is found across the Indo-European world, from India to Iceland. The particular version on which Tolkien drew most is the Norse tradition, as recounted by the mediaeval Icelandic poet and folklorist, Snorri Sturluson. *The Silmarillion* has even stronger and closer ties – for example, Beren the One-Handed recalls the Norse Tyr *Einhandr Ás* 'one-handed god'.

ɛ

Tolkien professed his dislike of allegory in the Preface to *The Lord of the Rings*, while simultaneously embracing myth and the mythic mode of narration throughout most of the tale. Both myth and allegory can be described as 'symbolic manipulation' – exploring relationships and ideas through symbols. The difference between the effect of each is partly due to the intentions of the author – allegory is narrowly and minutely determined by the writer, for example, leaving the reader little to do but act as a bystander. The effect is analytical, whereas with myth – properly handled for an audience in tune with the writer – it is an emotional experience.

For many readers, the experience of following the book through from Hobbiton down to Mordor and back to Hobbiton and onto the Grey Havens is deeply satistfying. Tolkien managed to tap into a need for myth in the modern, Western reader and to supply it in such an engaging way that the majority of readers probably never think about why they are so moved by the tale. We shall return to this aspect of his work in Chapter 6.

3. The Legacy of Heorot

Part of Tolkien's genius in creating *The Lord of the Rings* lies in grounding his mythology in reality. Although much of *The Hobbit* is lifted from a variety of northern legends, with a definite authorial twist to suit his personal style and intended audience, this is less true of *The Lord of the Rings* where a lot of the narrative is his own (sub-)creation.

He was very adept at taking usable elements from elsewhere and re-cycling them: the Elf-name Galdor is both Elvish 'shining lord' and Old English 'enchantment'; Orthanc and Mordor are others which existed before he adapted them. In one of his academic essays, Tolkien mentioned the peculiar effect of an unremarkable English word such as 'cellar-door' as a beautiful, melodious name: "Selador". This ear for the music of the language stood him in good stead when devising names for the characters and places in Middle-Earth.

The world in which he based his tale is one he knew well: the world of ancient northern myth and legend, and of the early English and their neighbours. The following are some examples of such aspects of his work, and the sources upon which he drew.

The Names, Places and Races of Middle-earth

One of the great strengths of Tolkien's work is that not only do the people and places have coherent and consistent names, but this practice extends even to details such as horses and swords. This is in keeping with the tales of mediaeval Iceland – where every hero bears a sword of repute – but is contrary to the English usage, as far as our existing records go. There are only two named swords in Old English literature: Beowulf's *Nægling*, and *Hrunting* lent to him by Hunferþ the Dane. In *The Lord of the Rings*, many of the important characters carry named weapons: Gandalf's sword *Glamdring* and Aragorn's *Narsil (Anduril)* – even Bilbo's *Sting*. The swords of the Rohirrim are, of course, given Old English names: Theoden's is called *Herugrim* 'grim sword'[1] or Eomer's *Guthwine* 'battle-friend'. The mighty ram used to smash the gates of Minas Tirith was named *Grond*, which is related to the OE *grindan* 'grind, crush, smash'.

Tolkien clearly felt that important objects should have histories, bound up with their identities and expressed in their unique names. Below are listed some of the more important persons, places and themes of the story with some suggestions as to sources and analogues in the worlds of mythology and history.

---

[1] There is an Old English word *heorugrimm* 'savage, fierce' of which *herugrim* would be the Mercian cognate. Tolkien habitually preferred Mercian over West Saxon forms.

"All Creation Wept"

After the fight with the Nazgûl, some Riders return to take away the bodies of Thedoen and Eowyn, but the others they leave in place with a hedge of spears round them, and they take the carcass of the beast and burn it. Rain begins to fall, extinguishing the Orcs' fires, as if everything is weeping for Eowyn and Theoden.

This motif is an ancient one in northern tradition. In Norse myth, the goddess Frigg asks all creation to swear not to harm her son, Baldur, but through the wiles of the trickster god, Loki, Baldur is slain by his blind brother. Then Frigg begs the goddess Hel – queen of the realms of death – for her son's return. This she will grant if Frigg can secure the agreement of all creation to weep for Baldur. Needless to say, Loki will not weep and the god must remain with Hel.

Amon Hen

Amon Hen is a place from which one can look out over many lands. Its name means 'hilltop of the eye'. It resembles the seat known as *Hliðskjalf* in Norse mythology, a place where Odin erected his seat from which he can over see all the nine worlds of creation. (see also *Barad-dûr*)

Anduril

see *Broken Sword*

Approval with Weapons

When the Riders of the Mark reach Gondor, Theoden addresses his men, urging them on to glory for the oaths they have sworn, the Riders respond by clashing their spears upon their shields.

The practice of signalling approval with weapons is of some antiquity. In Anglo-Saxon areas of the country, local groupings are called 'hundreds'; in the corresponding areas of the Danelaw, these are known as 'weapontakes' from the Norse *vapnatak* 'weapon-taking', the brandishing of weapons at a meeting to show assent to a proposal.

The Roman writer Tacitus, in *Germania 11*, writes of the Germans of the first century AD assembling to make communal decisions. If they disapprove of a proposal, they shout their dissent: if they approve, they clash their spears.

Aragorn

see also *Dúnedain*

Aragorn is the greatest traveller and hunter of his time, and being of Numenorean descent has a lifespan three times that of other Men.

Aragorn is a powerful blend of the mythic, the legendary and the historical. His approximation to the mythic hero-king was discussed in Chapter 2.

His name is based on (or influenced by) the name of the mediaeval Spanish kingdom or Aragon.

He resembles the legendary kings of old in certain key respects - his wisdom and pragmatism, his energetic defence of his people, his keen sense of justice. He walks among his folk as a common man, as some mediaeval kings are supposed to have done.

In terms of historical figures, there are not many early English kings whose life-stories are known in sufficient detail for a comparison to be made. However, there is one king of Wessex whose tale coincides with Aragorn's in more than one respect: King Alfred the Great.

Alfred was born into a royal family, but without any prospect of achieving kingship. (In Alfred's case this was due to having many older brothers.)	Aragorn was born into a royal family, but without any prospect of achieving kingship. (In Aragorn's case this was due to the kingdom's decline.)
Alfred spent a part of his life on the run in the wilderness of the Somerset marshes.	Aragorn was for many years a Dunedain Ranger living rough in the wilderness of Arnor.
Alfred overcame his foes in a series of battles, and arranged a political settlement with the remainder to secure his borders.	Aragorn fought the forces of Mordor, then agreed treaties with the Southrons and Easterlings to secure the peace.
Alfred's reign was a period of resurgence in English learning and cultural activity	Aragorn's reign is characterised by the repair and restoration of the greatness and symbolism of Gondor

However, Aragorn fights his war to achieve kingship while Alfred's greatest troubles came after he became king.

Aragorn is often compared to the other rulers in the tale: Denethor (lord of Gondor) and Theoden (king of the Rohan). In Tolkien's scheme, Denethor loses heart due to his pride and typifies the 'bad' heathen king, over-ambitious and manipulative. Theoden, by contrast, symbolises the 'good' heathen whose valour and loyalty win out over his misgivings. Within this scheme, Aragorn is closest to the 'Christian' king who combines the wisdom and subtlety of Denethor with the prowess and courage of Theoden, coupled with his own virtues – humility, doggedness, and patience.

At the Battle of Pelennor Fields, Aragorn wears a diadem on his brow in which is set the Star of the North Kingdom. The (spontaneous) appearance of a star on an individual's forehead is a sign of royal status in many northern European folktale traditions. Aragorn also received a brooch from Lothlorien set with a green gem, an Elf-stone; on his accession to the kingdom, he took the royal title *Elessar*, which means 'Elf-stone'. The word occurs in both English (Elphinstone) and German (Elbenstein) as a family name; the reference may perhaps be to the Elf-shot which was found in ploughed fields – Neolithic arrowheads of polished stone.

Several genuine English kings had names of this type. Most notable are 'elf-advice' (OE *ælf ræd*, Alfred) and 'noble stone' (OE *æðele stan*, Athelstan).

Aragorn's Song

On the way to Theoden's court, Aragorn begins to sing a song of the ancient north which the Rohirrim chant in the evening.

Aragorn's song is based directly on the Old English poem *The Ruin* in which a poet reflects on the transience of human life. Surveying the ruins of an ancient town (probably to be identified with the Roman remains at Bath, Somerset), he wonders where the inhabitants who made the proud city have gone to. Although they raised an impressive place, their memory has all but faded. The halls and chambers which once echoed to mirth and human voices now stand empty and desolate. The so-called '*ubi sunt*?' ("where are they?") passage is rephrased here for the house of Rohan. The elegiac tone and alliterative metre of the Old English verse is mimicked in Tolkien's imagery and style.

Arwen

We first meet Arwen at the feast in Rivendell where Frodo is presented to the assembly. She is a beautiful Elf-woman with dark hair and grey eyes.

Arwen Undomiel ("Evenstar") crafted a banner for Aragorn, to be used by him in the War of the Ring, and she reminded him of the prophecy concerning the Paths of the Dead. The idea of the noblewoman as a weaver is found throughout the Germanic world: both as the literal producer of textiles for the household and for trade, and as a figurative 'weaver of peace' (OE *friþuwebbe*) being given as a bride to unite warring families.

Athelas

After the escape from Moria, Sam's head-wound and Frodo's bruised ribs begin to slow them down. Aragorn examines Sam's cut and pronounces that it will heal if tended and treated with *athelas*, a herb of which he has a small supply of its dried leaves.

Athelas is the plant – a disregarded weed known as *kingsfoil* – which has very powerful healing properties in the right hands (the hands of a true king). Aragorn uses it to heal Frodo on Weathertop, and Faramir and Eowyn in Minas Tirith. It is derived from the Old English word *æðele* 'noble, high-born' (but *las* is an Elvish word for 'leaf' so this should be considered a word, like Orthanc or Mordor, which is well-formed in both Old English and Elvish).

Bag End

The naming of the road where Bilbo lives is a bilingual joke, of course, as well as a gentle snipe at pretentiousness: the name for a suburban spur from a road, serving only to give access to the houses sited round it, is the French term *cul de sac*, which Tolkien could not resist re-Englishing as Bag End.

Balrog

In the last stages of their flight from Moria, Frodo sees a black shape in the host of advancing Orcs. It is man-shaped but vast, and with a sword and whip of flame in its hands. This 'Balrog' is a spirit of fire from the beginning of time, imprisoned in the earth and unwittingly released by the digging of the Dwarves in Moria.

The closest mythical parallel to the Balrog is the demonic fire-giant Surtr of Norse tradition, whose coming heralds the ending of the world. He wields a fiery sword, and storms the rainbow bridge Bifrost which leads to heaven, just as Gandalf grapples with the Balrog on the bridge of Khazâd-dum.

Barad-dûr

The Barad-dûr or Black Tower is the centre of Sauron's power in Mordor. It is a huge, towering edifice from the top of which Sauron's lidless eye searches the many lands of Middle-Earth for the Ring which was once his. In this respect it resembles the Norse Hliðskjalfi discussed above under Amon Hen.

Barrows and Barrow-Wights

The 'barrows' of the story are based closely on the burial mounds (OE *beorgas*, our 'barrows') of Anglo-Saxon England. These were of two types: some were purpose built by the Anglo-Saxons themselves to house their important leaders – such would include the many mound-burials known from the royal gravefield at Sutton Hoo, Suffolk. Otherwise, they re-used existing mounds, usually of Bronze Age date, by placing their own dead in and around the structures; this may have been a symbolic claiming of the ancestral past of their recently acquired territories in Britain. The pre-existing monuments to the dead do not seem to have frightened the early English, but they remained keen to capture the power they felt resided within them.

The Anglo-Saxon mounds are usually circular in plan and sub-conical in profile. They are raised over a single burial which was often placed in a timber structure – famously, a 90 foot ship was used in Mound 1, Sutton Hoo. By contrast, the earlier (pre-Iron Age) mounds are often rectangular ("long-barrows") and many have a stone-built access area let into one end, where burials were made over several generations. Barrows of this type are found on Salisbury plain and in many other places throughout the British Isles where suitable stone occurs. With the coming of Christianity, it goes without saying that all such places were dismissed as heathen burials and became places of taboo. They remained in use for the execution of criminals and the burial of unbaptised people, and thus they acquired a reputation as the haunts of ghosts, witches and evildoers. By the time mediaeval legendary tradition had got to work on them, they had become entrances to the world of the dead – which was often their original purpose, after all – and the gateways to perilous realms from which men never returned unscathed. They eventually dwindled to become the 'hollow hills' of local legend.

The Barrow Downs strongly recall the alignments and clusters of monuments on the Berkshire Downs and elsewhere. These are often sited not on the crest of the hill but on the skyline, in order to have the maximum visual impact when seen from the inhabited river-valleys below.

In Scandinavian tradition, the dead were believed to linger in their mounds, sometimes continuing a form of spiritual existence there. Men might visit the barrow of their family in order to ask advice of their dead forebears, or even sleep on the mound so that they could receive prophetic dreams. Any object taken from a barrow would necessarily be both ancient and supernatural; ancient weapons especially were prized for their mettle and reputation, and some were believed to have been made by the Dwarves or the divine smith, Welund (Völund, Wayland). The way to the world of the dead was always 'northwards and downwards' in northern myth, just as Frodo's was.

In *Beowulf*, the lone survivor of a dwindling race hoards up his people's wealth in a gravemound before he too passes into death. Tolkien's portrayal of barrows in *The Lord of the Rings* agrees well with the early mediaeval attitude: they are ancient, sinister and associated with groups of men long gone. These men become in time mere 'creatures' – OE *wihtas*, 'beings, creatures' modern 'wights' – their humanity having been long forgotten. They lingered as guardians of the mounds and their contents, and were associated with weaving protective spells which would curse whoever removed the treasures from within.

Frodo and his companions confront the barrow-wight in his grave-mound. This is the first instance of the 'descent into the dark' theme in the book. Only Frodo does not fall victim to the hypnotic spell of the barrow-wight; he rather takes up arms and confronts his fear. In so doing he wins the prize of weapons for himself and his friends.

Barrows of Rohan

In the pursuit of Merry and Pippin, just inside Fangorn Forest, Aragorn finds a clearing where a great pyre has been made, with the Orcs' broken weapons stacked alongside it. Further off there is a newly-built mound, with fifteen spears stuck in the earth around it.

The barrows raised by the Riders over their fallen comrades are a symbol of the eternal fame and fond memory of the dead within. The spears lodged in the earth are a memorial to the fallen Riders. This use of barrows within a living tradition contrasts with the 'barrow-wights' episode where the wights are hostile guardians of wasted treasures, like the dragon in *Beowulf*.

Bilbo Baggins

Bilbo was the hero of the book *The Hobbit*. After his adventures with Gandalf and a group of Dwarves, he returned to the Shire with some gold and a ring which could make its wearer invisible. He lived alone in Bag End until, at a farewell party, he used the Ring to suddenly disappear. After that he left the Ring and his wealth for Frodo and set out to satisfy his *wanderlust*. Eventually Bilbo arrived in Rivendell where he lived a simple life writing history, and composing verse.

The name Bilbo Baggins was chosen by Tolkien for the main character in what was intended to be a whimsical children's story. There have been several suggestions as to the origin of the names. One refers the forename to the medieval word *bilbo* which means a type of sword (manufactured in Bilbao, Spain). Another brings in the geographical feature called Long Bilbo, a hill in the West Midlands. A third looks rather to an error in a mediaeval manuscript which gives *Bilba* as the name of the father of the Mercian King Penda (a misreading of Wibba?). Baggins is a country dialect word for a light meal or picnic.

The most likely explanation for the name is actually rather ordinary: that Tolkien just liked the playfully alliterative sound of it, and thought it suited the rather frivolous character of the hobbit before his many escapades changed him forever.

Black Breath

At the Battle of Pelennor Fields, Eowyn drives her blade into the void between the foe's shoulders and crown. The sword breaks apart, the crown falls to the ground and Eowyn collapses. She appears to be dead but is a victim of the Black Breath.

The Black Breath recalls the Last Battle between Gods and Giants at the Ragnarok. Þorr the mighty thunder-god manages to defeat the Miðgarðsomr – the huge serpent which encircles the world – but he takes just nine paces from the combat, then falls dead to the ground, overcome by the poison of the creature's breath.

Black Riders

see *Ringwraiths*

Black Tower

see *Barad-dûr*

Bombadil

See *Old Man Willow*

Tom Bombadil is one of the more contentious figures in *The Lord of the Rings*. Some readers do not warm to him at all, and find the adventures in his woods an irrelevant diversion which does nothing to further the main story. Yet Tolkien clearly liked Tom and his partner Goldberry, and felt them worth including in the book (they had already been published in a book of his verse).

Some critics have seen in them a pair of nature spirits, of woods and river respectively, although this seems unsatisfactory to those readers who look for analogues in mythology. The pair do appear to be guardians of the land around them, and Goldberry has a special affinity with running water and plant-life, but they are not bound to it in the way that Treebeard, for example, is bound to Fangorn Forest. Neither does Tom have any of the powerful, awe-inspiring qualities one would normally associate with nature-divinities – the chaotic vivacity, the alarming unpredictable potency. Although he may retain traces of some past divinity in his mastery of the land and all it contains, his resistance to the Ring and his use of song and spells, the effect conveyed by the character is of puckish exuberance. Bombadil's Elvish name, *Forn*, is an Old English word meaning 'ancient, original' and indeed Gandalf says that he was the first all of creatures on Middle-Earth.

Tom's speech is heavily rhythmic, not exactly poetry but bound to the rhyming patterns of verse. In this respect it recalls some Old English literature where there is plain prose and highly-wrought alliterative verse, and also a rhythmic, ornate style of prose writing which mimics some features of the formal verse.

Tolkien characterised Tom as the spirit of pure intellect, concerned only with finding out and understanding, but not with using the knowledge gained for any purpose. In this respect, and in his singing and love of cheerful colours, Tom Bombadil is probably no more than one facet of Tolkien himself. For that reason he must always feel like an intrusion into the world of myth.

In the poem *Bombadil Goes Boating* the tale is told of his meeting with Goldberry, the Riverwoman's daughter. There are elements of Norse myth in this poem, specifically the story of the Nibelung treasure, and how the curse laid on it by Andvari brought destruction to all who acquired it. (This story was adapted by Richard Wagner into the famous *Ring der Nibelungen* operatic cycle.) It is unclear who the Riverwoman is intended to be, although the Norse god of the sea, Ægir, has a wife called Ran who shares his aquatic hall. Goldberry appears to be a river-spirit, perhaps like the Lorelei and various other beautiful but perilous aquatic females.

Boromir

The story of Boromir and Faramir is familiar from a series of myths where two or more brothers are set a task, and the youngest (or smallest, or weakest) is the only one to succeed. The test in *The Lord of the Rings* is the rejection of temptation – the power of the Ring is well-known but so is its danger. The lure of the Ring is too much for Boromir, who is exposed to it over a lengthy period. Faramir manages to resist the temptation to seize and wield it for the short while Frodo is in his power.

Boromir regretted his temporary loss of control and fought bravely defending Merry and Pippin. That he was redeemed by his action (and forgiven by his companions) is suggested by the fact that later his body appeared in a boat floating on the river, wreathed in light.

Tolkien adapted elements from the mythic theme of the Divine Twins in which usually one brother is heroic and adventurous and the other is dedicated to the parents and the farm. The adventurous one prospers through a series of daring escapades, while the slower one falls into oblivion. The pair often undertake a mission to recapture an abducted female relative. Tolkien's Boromir : Faramir pairing makes use of a small part of this rich mythic seam.

Boundary Stone

The army of Rohan approaches Isengard from Helm's Deep, where the former grassy valley has become a wasteland of brambles and tree-stumps, with steam rising and smoke lying in the dells. A pillar looms before them, black and embellished with the sign of the White Hand, which is Saruman's badge.

The boundary marker is reminiscent of large standing-stones which were used to mark off territory in Anglo-Saxon times. Many date from the Neolithic period and were probably originally objects of veneration. The Anglo-Saxons found them very prominent features, which were virtually immobile and therefore useful as fixed points for demarcating boundaries.

Bree

Having been rescued by Tom Bombadil from the barrow-wights, Tom advises them to travel without stopping to the inn of the Prancing Pony, in the village of Bree, which is a mixed community of men and hobbits.

The village name 'Bree' is a Celtic word meaning 'hill'. The village is referred to as 'Bree under Bree-hill' which is logically nonsense (hill under hill-hill?). It is however typical of English place-names in the west, that they retain traces of pre-English (Brythonic Celtic) language. Pendle Hill is another example of the phenomenon: originally British *pen* 'hill, high point, head' to which the early English added *hyll* 'hill'; OE *penhyll* became in time *pendle* which no longer meant anything to English-speakers, so 'hill' was added again: Pendle Hill.

Nearly all the place-names of the Bree-land have a Celtic flavour, so that they seem familiar but don't appear to mean anything, much like the place-names of western England which retain a strong element of British. Chetwood, for example, combines Welsh *chet* 'wood' with the explanatory English '-wood'.

Broken Sword

see also *Isildur* & *Melted Sword*

Aragorn is the owner of the heirloom sword *Narsil* which was shattered in the first war with Sauron. During his stay at Rivendell, it is re-forged for him and re-named *Anduril* 'flame of the west'.

The motif of a broken sword, an heirloom which is subsequently reforged, is drawn from the partly-mythic legend of the Volsungs, where the hero Sigurð assists Reginn the smith in repairing *Gram*, his family weapon.

Camps in Mordor

See *Mordor*

Cock-Crow

see *Horn Blast*

Cormallen Field

In the battle outside the Black Gate, where the Army of the West is beleaguered on its two hilltop positions, Gandalf cries out to halt a counter-attack which would leave them exposed.

There may be an echo here of the stand of the English army atop the ridge at Senlac, where it is alleged that an incautious commander failed to stop his men pursuing the retreating Norman cavalry down the hill. Duke William's horsemen quickly turned and rode the infantry down, and the English army was fatally weakened. The battle and its date are among the best known in English history: Hastings, 1066.

Cracks of Doom

Approching the summit of Mount Doom, Frodo and Gollum fight but Frodo throws the attacker off then clutches at the Ring beneath his shirt and tells Gollum that if he ever touches him again he shall be cast into the fires at the Crack of Doom.

The phrase 'Cracks of Doom' is part of mediaeval Christian mythology, where it refers to the breaking of the heavens at the coming of the last day, the Judgement Day. Tolkien adapted the phrase into a physical feature of the volcanic mountain at the heart of Mordor.

Cremation

see *Heathen Kings*

Dark Lord

see *Sauron*

Dead Marshes

In the Dead Marshes, Frodo and Sam catch a glimpse of luminescence way off in the marsh, which Gollum calls "tricksy lights". Sam discovers that below the surface there are images of dead faces, pale and lifeless – some evil-looking, some of noble appearance, but all dead and rotting. They are remnants of the battle fought there between Men and Elves and Orcs, long ages before.

Hereward, the English resistence fighter, was based on the Isle of Ely, surrounded by fen and marshland. William of Normandy had a timber causeway built, about a mile long, so as to bring his troops close enough to storm Ely. As the Norman force crossed the causeway it sank into the marsh, causing many of them to drown. The subsidence may have been due to the weight of a large number of troops, or the handiwork of the defenders. Whatever the reason, it is said that the bodies of the invaders lay submerged and rotting in the marshes for years after the event.

The vision of the will o' the wisp and the images of rotting corpses may have been inspired by Tolkien's experiences in the trenches in World War I where the bodies of both sides often lay side-by-side in death. The fact that there are both fair and foul among them may be Tolkien's way of reminding us that no matter which side we are on, we all come to the same end in time.

Decision Making

Denethor sends a messenger to Rohan, asking for help, but King Theoden questions the messenger since the Rohirrim fight from horseback on open land not from behind walls. The king agrees that his army will come to Gondor's aid but offers the messenger a night's lodgings before returning. He proposes to give his final decision in the morning.

The Roman writer Tacitus remarks in his work *Germania* of the Germanic folk of his time that they thought it best to debate important issues at a feast where there was strong drink and men were less able to hide their feelings, but that decision-making was left till the next morning when they were sober and cool-headed.

Denethor

We meet Denethor only at the end of his life, in the final few days before despair and dismay finally overthrow his reason. Having used the *palantir* (seeing-stone) to try to learn of Sauron's plans, he was shown only those images that the Dark Lord wished him to see – the might of Mordor. This led him to believe that there was no real prospect of victory against such overwhelming odds. The final vision in the seeing-stone of a fleet of black-sailed ships sailing up the Anduin broke what little courage remained within him, and he decided to take his own life.

This motif is presumably adapted from the Greek story of Theseus: the hero set out to slay the minotaur in a black-sailed ship and promised to raise a white sail for his homecoming if he were successful; in his haste to return, he forgot his promise, and his father, on seeing the black sail appear on the horizon, threw himself off the cliff to his death.

Dernhelm

Watching as the Rohirrim prepare to ride, Merry is approached by a youth who offers him a seat on his horse, hidden beneath the rider's cloak. Merry gladly accepts and asks the Rider's name, which he gives as Dernhelm. Seated on his horse, *Windfola*, the Rider joins the troop as they ride out.

Dernhelm is OE *derne* 'secret' + *helm* 'helmet'. The helmet conceals the Rider's identity. *Windfola* is *wind* 'wind' + *fola* 'foal'.

Descent into Darkness - Moria

The Fellowship, having been beaten back from the Pass of Caradhras, descend from the mountain to pass through the mines of Moria, led by Gandalf.

The passage through Moria is is an example of 'descent into the dark' mythic theme. The journey through the mines and halls is gruelling and holds many dangers, but the 'pay-off' comes at the confrontation with the Balrog. Gandalf fights the creature and suffers his own 'descent into the dark' beneath the earth where he strives against the Balrog, and finally they destroy each other. Yet a prize is won there: Gandalf's destruction leads to his being sent back in a more powerful form, an 'escape from death' (or a resurrection) unlike any other in the book.

Descent into Darkness – Mount Doom

At the summit of Mount Doom Frodo renounces the quest and claims the Ring for himself. He puts it onto his finger and disappears from sight.

Frodo's final 'descent into the dark' on Mount Doom is the turning point for the whole tale, and results in the winning of the greatest prize: the overthrow of the Dark Lord and all his works. However, since Frodo was ultimately unable to let the Ring go voluntarily, he has not actually shed his burden and therefore, for him, the victory is incomplete. He is to be tormented by the memory of these events and his longing for the Ring, until he passes into *the West*.

Descent into Darkness

See also *Paths of the Dead*

Devouring Wolf

The motif Sam alludes to when, camped below Caradhras and surrounded by wargs, he says Gandalf is not likely to end up in any wolf's belly, is found in Norse mythology, where the gods march out at the Ragnarökr, the Last Day, to face their foes: giants, serpents and wolves. The god Óðinn leads his army forth from his hall Valhöll and fights Fenrir, the giant wolf whom the gods previously tricked into fetters. The wolf swallows the god and, significantly, his son Váli thc avenger places one foot in the wolf's lower jaw and forces the beast's mouth open to release his father.

According to advocates of the 'nature myth' school of interpretation, the wolf represents the night and the sun-god disappears into his belly only to reappear the next morning.

Dúnedain

The Dúnedain are the Rangers of *The Lord of the Rings*, a race of men who have descended from the Númenorians. In that sense, their finest days are already over as the tale begins; yet the events of the War of the Ring demonstrate that they have a great future ahead of them also.

The Dúnedain are the Men of the West, the only High Men still to be found in Middle-Earth. Their leader, Elendil, founded two kingdoms for them: the northern realm of Arnor (noble land) and the southern of Gondor (land of stone). The rulership of Gondor passed into the hands of stewards, whose position became hereditary like the kingship it replaced. The kingdom of Arnor failed, and its last inhabitants became itinerant folk who nevertheless retained the memory of their ancestry and maintained Númenorean traditions.

They were known to other peoples as Rangers. Aragorn, leader of the Rangers, passes from a homeless 'cowboy' drifter to a position of responsibility within the Fellowship, and ultimately to kingship. In the pursuit of the captured hobbits, he demonstrates his keen tracking skills learnt from years in the wild.

Dunharrow

See *Púkel-men*

Dunharow (Old English *dun* 'hill' and *hearh* 'temple, place of worship') is a fortress refuge reached by a path which climbs a steep cliff, winding back and forth. At each turn there is a standing stone carved in the likeness of a man, squatting with folded arms. They are called Púkel-men by the Riders of Rohan but their tale is unknown. The top of the cliff is reached by passing through a wall out onto the *Firienfeld*. Behind are mountains called Starkhorn, Irensaga and Dwimorberg; two parallel lines of standing stones point towards the latter, leading into the Dimholt (a stand of gloomy woodland) and the entrance to the Paths of the Dead. Dunharrow was made by men long-forgotten and the Rohirrim have no legends of how it came to be.

Púkel-men. *Pucel* or the variant *puca* is an Old English term for a goblin or brownie. See *Pukel-men*

Firienfeld is Old English and means open land *'feld'* on a mountain or high place *'fyrgen'*. Dimholt is likewise OE *dimm holt* "dark wood".

The mountains are named from OE *stearc horn* 'strong horn', *dwimmor berg* 'ghost rock', *iren sagu* 'iron saw'; the latter is a many-pointed mass of rock.

The rows of standing-stones recall the linear monuments of Britain – perhaps the winding avenue at Avebury.

Dunlendings

The Dunlendings are Men who fought on the side of the Orcs in the battle at Isen fords.

The Dunlendings were the wildmen whom the Rohirrim had ejected from the plain of Rohan, and who continued to fight the Horse-lords for control of the territory. The name may be Old English for 'highlanders' from *dun* 'down, hill' and *land*, or else the first element might be *dun* 'dun, tan, pale brown'.

The Dunlendings were not the same folk as the original builders of Dunharrow.

Dwarves.

Tolkien's Dwarves are a short, sturdy and tireless race of miners, masons and metalworkers. Their skill is in fashioning hard materials into beautiful shapes as distinct from the softer textile crafts of the Elves. They could be implacable foes, jealous of their rights, holding grudges for generations and reluctant to make concessions. Their womenfolk are few and their procreative arrangements are a mystery. Indeed, much of the internal life of the race is hidden from outsiders: they never reveal their 'true' names to anyone, nor allow them to be recorded; they use a unique script (the Cirth – see Chapter 4 *Language; Writing; The Cirth*); they dwell underground and have adapted their lifestyle to a subterranean existence.

The place of the Dwarves in English and Norse mythology is ambiguous. They seem distant or aloof from the affairs of men in the tales, amenable to helping if an incentive were on offer, but not really involved. Their strongest associations are with mining and metalwork: the Dwarves Brokk and Sindri forged treasures for the gods of Ásgard such as the hammer, Mjolnir, which Þórr (Thor) wielded. They were devious and clever, with a strong tradition of exchange and private ownership. The Dwarves may be identical with the *svartálfar* of Norse myth – the 'dark Elves', who are swarthy, ugly and ill-tempered. They were formed in the earth by two elders, Motsognir and Durinn – hence Tolkien's use of the name Durin for the dwarvish ancestor in The *Hobbit.* Many of the Dwarf-names in *The Hobbit* occur in the Norse *Dvergatal* poem.

The word 'Dwarf' is based on the Old English *dweorg,* which is associated with certain kinds of feverish illness. (Elves were likewise associated with sudden pain or 'stitch', as in the Old English charm *Wið Færsticce* 'Against Sudden Stitch'. They were further connected with other sudden ailments, such as hiccups (*ælfsogoða*).) If the word had been in everyday use in English, it would have evolved the by-form *dwerrow* (as *beorg* became 'barrow' or *hearg* became 'harrow'). This explains the name Dwerrowdelf – 'delving of the Dwarves'.

Dwarves are the metalworkers and smiths of legend, people with skills which were essential to success of all communities from the dawn of the Bronze Age onwards. Smiths themselves were frequently itinerant outsiders with the god-like skill of turning earth into metal through the use of air and fire.

Their livelihoods rested on their ability to barter their products for food, shelter and other services. It may be in this relationship of metalworkers to their customers that the traditional greed and possessiveness of the Dwarves was born.

Tolkien hardly had to adapt the Germanic lore of the Dwarves at all to bring them to life in the pages of his books.

Earendil

Earendil was a seafarer who sailed the coasts of Middle-Earth and out onto the western ocean. He married Elwing Half-elven who gave him a crown surmounted by a *silmaril*. When his ship was blown out into the land of the Valar, he was transformed into an immortal being who would sail the night sky forever, and the light from his crown was to be a symbol of permanence and hope for the peoples of Middle-Earth.

The name *Earendil* occurs in Old English documents, where it refers to a celestial object, possibly Venus the morning star. However, Tolkien knew that there was a long tradition behind the name, since it occurs in a Norse tale of the god Þórr (Thor). One day, crossing a river, the god carried a Dwarf named Aurvandil over the flood in a basket. One of the Dwarf's toes protruded and due to the extreme cold, was frozen solid. Þórr broke the toe off and threw it up into the heavens where it became a star. (*Aurvandil* is the Norse form of the name which occurs as *Earendil* in Old English.) In German tradition, furthermore, the hero *Orentil* (another form of the name) was a prince who suffered shipwreck and won a bride called *Breide* (bright).

Current scholarly opinion suggests that the word is based on an ancient Germanic compound **auso-wandilaz* 'dawn-wanderer'. The root **auso-* is the basis of the English words 'east' (where the sun rises) and 'Easter' (spring festival) as well as Latin *aurora* 'dawn'. The root **wand-* is present in modern English 'wander', 'wind' and 'wend'.

Tolkien drew together the various strands – the heroic life, the association with ships and water, the transformation into a celestial body – and worked them into a fresh story of his own. This technique was typical of his approach to the creative use of ancient material: he made something new and complete from broken fragments of legend scattered in the literature of several peoples.

Edoras

See also *Meduseld*

Where a stream comes down from the White Mountains there is a hill protected by ditch, wall and palisade; behind the defences stand many buildings: that is Edoras, the seat of the kings of Rohan. On a flat, grassy bank there stands apart a large hall thatched with gold: *Meduseld*, the king's hall. Because of the golden decoration on the timber and thatch, there shines a light over the surrounding land. Mail-clad warriors patrol the walls.

Edoras is the name of the court where King Theoden rules. The word is plural; the standard singular is *eodor* 'shelter'; *Edoras* therefore means 'sheltering places'.

Eldamar

See *Númenor*

Eleventy-One

The unusual numeral has raised a few eyebrows, being regarded as 'cute' or childish. It is however not without historical foundation. The Anglo-Saxons used a decimal number system, the ancestor of our own. However, there were elements of the system that were not based on a simple 'tens-and-units' organisation. There were traces of an older principle based on groups of twelve.

For one thing, the numbers from one to ten are unanalysable but 'eleven' and 'twelve' are *endleofon*, *twelf* and ultimately reflect **ain-leb-* , **twai-leb-* '(ten and) one-left, two-left'. Thereafter the series runs *þreotiene* 'three (plus) ten' and so on. The numbers eleven and twelve are an anomaly.

Likewise, the decades from 70 up to 120 could be prefixed with the word *hund-* so that seventy was *hundseofontig*, eighty *hundeahtatig*, ninety *hundnigonty*, a hundred *hundteontig* (i.e. ten-ty). a hundred and ten *hundendlufontig* (eleven-ty) and *hundtwelftig* (twelve-ty). (These numerals occur in King Alfred's translation of Orosius; elsewhere, *hund* meant one hundred, and the series then ran from there with the normal numerals.)

From this it is reasonable to deduce that *eleventy-one* would have been a possible description of the numeral 111, if the Alfredian system had remained in use. Far from being mere whimsy, 'eleventy-one' is an actual old word that has fallen into disuse.

Elrond

Both Elrond and his twin brother Elros were 'half-elven' i.e. their ancestry contained both Men and Elves. Their father was Earendil, the seafarer who went on to become a star. The brothers faced a choice of adopting humanity and mortality, or assuming an immortal Elvish identity. Elros chose to be human, while Elrond chose immortality and went on to become the wisest of his race

There are many pairs of twins in European mythology, of which the most famous are probably Romulus and Remus in the Roman tradition, or Castor and Pollux (*Kastor* and *Polydeukes*) in the Greek. The death of one twin led to a significant transformation: the founding of the city of Rome for Romulus, and the transformation into the constellation *Gemini* for the Greek pair. Often, it was believed that one twin belonged to the human father and the other had been sired by a god: this may have given Tolkien the idea for the pairing of Man and Elf as siblings.

The English knew the myth also: the legendary founders of the Kingdom of Kent were two brothers called Hengest and Horsa ('stallion' and 'horse').

Elves

The Elves in *The Lord of the Rings* are Tolkien's attempt to put these beings back where they belong: at the heart of English myth and legend. In Germanic lore, Elves are shining creatures of immense beauty. Tolkien's Elves were taller than Men and graceful, with dark hair and grey eyes, except for the fair-haired 'golden house of Finrod'. While the Elves of Middle-Earth were powerful and well-intentioned, they were also aloof, dispassionate and suspicious. The Elves were associated most strongly with weaving and carving – 'feminine' skills against the mining and metalworking of the Dwarves. They had a long tradition of poetry, literature and story-telling.

Elves in Anglo-Saxon tradition are linked with both illness and cure. Certain common ailments were believed to be caused by the Elves: *ælfsogoða* 'Elf-sough' is hiccups, *ælfscot* 'Elf-shot' is the stabbing pain of rheumatism or arthritis, while *wæterælfadl* 'Water-Elf ailment' is chickenpox. Plants with healing properties include *ælfþone* 'elfthon, dogwood'.

While some Elves could be persuaded to assist with daily work for a small gift or offering, there were others who took pleasure in causing mishaps and ill-will. Likewise the Norse *ljósálfar* 'light-Elves' were on the side of gods and men against the giants and trolls, but still it could be dangerous for men to deal with them. In Irish tradition, the *Sidhe* folk[1] were likewise unpredictable; they had the use of magical powers, and could foresee the future. They lived in secret chambers underground, or beneath the sea.

The whiteness of the Elves, their inner luminescence, is also an ancient motif. The word 'Elf' (Old English *ælf*) means 'brilliant, white, shining' and is based on the same root as the words 'Alp' (White Mountains) and 'albumen' (white of an egg). In Old English a derived word is *ælfet* or *ielfet* 'swan', the shining white bird. A term of immense praise for a woman was to call her *ælfscienu* 'Elf-fair'.

Ents

In the forest of Fangorn, Merry and Pippin are confronted by a tall, gnarled creature with grey-green skin like bark, short twiggy arms, a mossy beard and deep brown-green eyes which hold them spellbound. The creature – which resembles a tree in many respects - announces that he is called Fangorn, or 'Treebeard' in their language, and that he is an Ent. The hobbits are in awe of him, but do not feel threatened. Treebeard is puzzled and unsure how to classify their kind among the living creatures known to him.

The Ents are the shepherds of the trees, and appear to be based on the folktales of unseen guardians who would take care of a wood, hill, stream or valley, and would avenge any damage done to it. These were known to the Romans as *genii loci* 'spirits of the place' and Roman soldiers were always

---

[1] The *Sidhe* (pronounced 'shee') are believed to be the remaining folk tradition concerning the Irish gods of the Iron Age, the *Túatha Dé Danaan.*

careful, when raising an altar, to placate both the high gods of their own pantheon and the local deities.

Tolkien's Ents are a blend of these protective nature spirits and the various kinds of giant beings which inhabited wild places in the folklore of the north. The missing Entwives are a twist on two strands of Scandinavian legend. The estrangement of the Ents from their females due to the love of wildwood and fields respectively echoes the disagreement between the Norse god Njorðr and his bride Skaði: he loved the sea while she could not be happy far from her mountain home, and they could not agree upon a site for their shared dwelling. The constant searching of the Ents for the Entwives recalls the Norse goddess Freyja who searched Middle-Earth for her estranged husband, Óðr. There is a hint (it is no more) in the book that the Entwives may one day be found: Sam recounts his cousin Hal's encounter with a walking beech tree in Book I, to the disbelief of his companions. Later, in Fangorn Forest, Treebeard asks whether any such creatures are ever seen in the Shire, as they would love that country.

Ent is an Old English word for 'giant' or 'mysterious being'. Roman ruins in the landscape were described as *eald enta geweorc* 'old works of the Ents'.

The metre of the Ent's rhyme is essentially that of Old English alliterative verse with its four-stressed line and alliteration of the first and/or second with the third stressed syllable. Interestingly, the phrase used to describe the bear ("bee-hunter") is a paraphrase of the name Beowulf i.e. bee-wolf, one who robs bees (of their honey), a kenning for 'bear'.

Eomer

Tracking Merry and Pippin and their Orc captors across the Plains of Rohan, Aragorn, Legolas and Gimli meet a group of horsemen who surround them and level their spears and arrows at the travellers; the leader, Eomer, demands to know who the strangers are and what business they have in Rohan.

Eomer is the first of the Horse-Lords to enter the tale directly. He deals boldly and fairly with the company. Eomer's position at the court of Theoden is unique, in that he is not just another member of the royal household, he is the king's sister's son. The relationship between mother's brother and sister's son was very special – almost sacred – in all Germanic societies. On her marriage, the bride went to live with her husband's people but her blood-kin continued to care for her and her children. Since she could not deal with her husband's people without risk of friction, it fell to her brother to protect her interests and those of her children. The mother's brother was a kind of 'legal guardian' as well as an adviser and substitute father figure for her sons.

Eored

The forces of Rohan are divided into groups of Riders, each under a section leader. Each such division is known as an *eored*, an Old English word meaning '(group of) horse-riders', from *eoh* 'horse'.

Eowyn the Shieldmaiden

Lady Eowyn begins as a tragic figure in *The Lord of the Rings*, a brave spirit caught in the body of a woman and thus banned from active participation in the struggle. Her unrequited love for Aragorn, and the bitterness of her kin, led her to despair of life and seek a glorious death. Her contest with the Nazgûl came close to killing her even though she managed to despatch her foe. However, Eowyn's tale took a further twist when she fell in love with Faramir during their convalescence. (One wonders whether Tolkien's experiences during his convalescence after trench fever was a factor here.)

Eowyn's passing herself off as a male warrior is an echo of the legendary shieldmaidens of northern literature: women whose proficiency with weapons allows them a place of honour among the warriors. They may originally have been devotees of the Woden-cult. The warrior-queen Brunhild in the *Nibelung Saga* is probably the most famous lady of this type – a perilous ice-maiden whom the hero must overcome and tame.

There is some evidence for weapon-bearing women in Anglo-Saxon times, although it is not plentiful. Tolkien seems to be recalling the Norse tradition of the *valkyrjar* (valkyries) who were imagined to be beautiful young women, dressed in armour, who would choose the bravest and boldest on the battlefield to be slain and carried off by them to Óðinn's hall, *Valhöll* (Valhalla). Old English recognised the concept in the words *wælceosig* (slain-choosing) describing a bird of prey, and *wæcyrige* (valkyrie, slain-chooser) which appears as a translation of the Greek Furies.

Fallohides

See *Hobbits*

Fangorn Forest

See *Ents*

Far-sighted Dreams

While staying in the house at Crickhollow, Frodo dreams of the sea and a tall, white tower which he yearns to climb.

Thus early in the tale Frodo sees himself climbing a tower looking over the western sea – almost the last incident in the book. It is never made explicit that Frodo's dream is prescient, but the evidence in the tale can be read in this way.

Prophetic dreams are a commonplace of mythic tales. Sometimes the dream misleads the hero, but more often it is a warning of bad luck to come. The Norse god Baldur was troubled by dreams of his own death, which prompted his mother, Frigg, to ensure that nothing would harm him. Enjoying his invulnerable state, he became the target of the gods' sport: they would throw weapons of every sort at him but he would suffer no injury. At last the trickster god Loki discovered that the mistletoe plant had not sworn the oath not to injure him, and he set about causing Baldur's death with a spear of this wood. The prophetic dream therefore fulfilled itself, since without it the oath would not have been taken and the game would never have been played.

Faramir

see also *Boromir*

Faramir is the younger son of Denethor, Steward of Gondor, and brother to Boromir.

While Boromir is a keen and able warrior, Faramir is less concerned with contests for their own sake, and more with the protection of the land he loves, Gondor. Faramir also has a deep respect for Gandalf. These facts in combination lead to his father's displeasure, and it comes as a harder blow then when Boromir, the favourite son, is slain.

In order to prove himself in his father's eyes, Faramir fights recklessly, earning the respect of the Men of Gondor, but his father's icy and reluctant acceptance. During the Seige of Minas Tirith he succumbs to the Nazgûl's Black Breath and Denethor, despairing at the loss of his second son, takes his own life. (see *Denethor*) However, Aragorn is able to cure Faramir, though he takes no further part in the War of the Ring. During his convalescence he falls in love with Eowyn of Rohan and the two are later married, joining the Houses of Gondor and Rohan.

Faramir's Raiders

While camping in Ithilien, Frodo and Sam meet brown- and green-clad strangers, armed with spears and bows.

The camouflage clothing, use of spears and bows, and general guerrilla tactics of this group are very reminiscent of Robin Hood and his men in English folklore. They must use stealth and carefully planned surprise attacks to harry their foe, in much the same way as Robin's men did. Ithilien is a fair land gone to ruin under the depredations of a merciless foreign invader, just as England was under Norman rule. Tolkien may have felt that the image of the greenwood and its defenders was too strong in English tradition to be omitted from his 'Mythology for England'.

Fates of the Rings of Power

The fates of the Rings of Power are recounted by Gandalf to the Council of Elrond, indicating the present balance of power in Middle-Earth: three rings were made for the Elves, but since Sauron was not permitted to touch them the Elves remain free and their works do not inevitably turn to evil. Seven were given to the Dwarves, but three have been regained by Sauron and four are destroyed, so that the Dwarves remain free of Sauron's corrupting will, but correspondingly unable to call on the potency of their rings. The nine which were given to Men enslaved those who wore them, turning them into Ringwraiths; they are unable to benefit from their treasures, since they no longer have any personal will or individual identity. Therefore: the leaders of Men are under Sauron's power, and the Dwarves have destroyed or lost their rings; the Elves remain outside his control, but Sauron need not fear the Elves if he can regain the Ruling Ring.

This hierarchy reflects the degree to which these races are given over to evil in the story, and corresponds quite well to the situation in traditional folktales.

"Ferthu Theoden hal!"

Before Theoden sets off for Gondor, Eowyn brings wine for the king, a leaving-cup, with the words *"Ferthu Theoden hal!"*.

Although not a recorded phrase from Old English, the wording means *"Go in health, Theoden!"* parallel to *westu hal* earlier. It is a manner of saying "farewell".

Flet

After the Fellowship escape from Moria, Legolas sings the song of the maiden Nimrodel who dwelt long ago beside the stream which bears her name. Like all the Elves of Lothlorien, she dwelt on a *flet* or platform built into the branches of a tree.

The word *flet* is Old English and is commonly used to mean 'raised or sprung wooden floor'.

"Forth Eorlingas!"

The cry *"Forth, Eorlingas*!", used by Theoden to spur on his troops, is pure Old English. *Eorlingas* is a folk-name of an ancient Germanic type in which the suffix *–ingas* denoting 'followers' is added to the leader's name, here 'Eorl'. The *Eorlingas* are thus the 'followers of Eorl', who was the first of the Rohirrim leaders in the Riddermark. The injunction 'forth' – or Old English *forð* – recalls the Old English poem *The Battle of Maldon* where the English army is exhorted to go *forð* to meet the Viking raiders.

The phrase therefore means "Forward, Eorl's men!".

Frodo Baggins

Frodo was the son of Drogo Baggins and Primula Brandybuck, adopted by his cousin Bilbo after they died. At Bilbo's 111st birthday party, the old hobbit suddenly vanished leaving most of his possessions, including his house and his magic ring, to Frodo. The Lord of the Rings is the tale of how Frodo takes the Ring to Mount Doom, where it is destroyed. When the task is completed and the War of the Ring has ended, Frodo will have nothing more to do with weapons and retires to Michel Delving in the Shire, but he is never able to overcome the craving for the Ring. He manages to escape death by passing into the Undying Lands in the West with Bilbo. At the beginning of his quest, in the house of Tom Bombadil, Frodo dreamt of that passage which could suggest that the course of events was already mapped out, although his story might be no more than one among many possibilities.

Frodo is a modernised form of the ancient name Froda, '(he who is) old and wise', a person of long experience. In Old English records, the name Froda is found in *Beowulf*. He was a king of the Heaðobeardan who died in the war between his folk and the Danes. His son, Ingeld, tried to patch up the quarrel with a marriage alliance, but this plan went awry.

The name is linked to the Danish tradition of the *froðafrið* 'peace of Froði'. Froði, the Norse form of Froda, was a mythical king of the Danes who owned a pair of magical millstones which could grind out whatever he desired: his reign was marked by riches, peace and plenty although he came to a bad end. Frodo's return to the shire is accompanied by bumper harvests and a spate of births and marriages.

Galadriel

The Lady Galadriel of Lothlorien was rare among the Elves in that she was fair-haired, a daughter of the 'golden house of Finrod'. She appears as a stronger and more important figure than her spouse, Celeborn, and she bears one of the Rings of Power.

In Lorien, she showed Frodo her Mirror, a vessel in which water could be poured to form a reflective surface. In this Mirror one could see the past, the present and a 'possible future', that is to say, she did not claim that what Frodo saw would *necessarily* come to be. The situation is perhaps similar to the foretelling of the three weird sisters in Macbeth, whose prophecies appear to mean one thing but in the end prove duplicitous.

Along with the ladies of her circle, Galadriel was accomplished in the elvish craft of weaving. The gifts of her court to the Fellowship included cloaks of grey which would disguise the wearer (not unlike the folktale motif of the 'cloak of invisibility', though the effect was closer to camouflage than true disappearance). While it may appear incongruous to us that a woman could be a gift-giver, there is a historical precedent in the Old English poem *Beowulf* where the young hero receives a set of splendid treasures from Queen Wealhþeow of the Danes, independently of her husband's gifts to him. There is also the folktale motif of the 'worthless gift' given by a mysterious female, such as a bunch of dead leaves which later turn out to be made of gold. Many of the gifts Galadriel gave were later significant in the tale.

In Germanic tradition there are many supernatural prophetic women associated with wells and with weaving; in historical times, these spaewives were important in religious and diplomatic matters, using their scrying powers to determine whether a proposed course of action would be favourable. The *Nornir* of Norse myth were three supernatural women who wove the fates of men on their loom of time, and whose other main task was to wash the trunk of the World Tree with water from the *Urðabrunnr* (Well of Weird). These women were also closely connected with feasting rituals, formal speeches and gift-giving and the drinking of ceremonial draughts: this feature is present in Galadriel's offering the Fellowship a parting cup before they say their farewells.

Gandalf

The wizards in *The Lord of the Rings* are a group of beings – less powerful than the Valar – who are sent into the world to unite the Free Peoples in their struggles against Sauron. There were five in all, though only three appear in the book: Saruman, Radagast and Gandalf. While Saruman locked himself away with his studies in his tower, Gandalf roamed the world teaching and advising, gathering news and learning about the less important folk of Middle-Earth. He appeared as an old man dressed in grey, with a broad hat and a handful of party tricks to entertain simple folk. In these respects he resembles Óðinn[1], who was often content to wander as an old man in simple garb and to learn the ways of men.

The order of wizards follows quite closely the model of these characters in European folktale. There is a suspicion that wizards are themselves distortions of original divine figures. In the Norse tale of King Víkarr, the king is assisted by an older and wiser character called Grani *Hrosshar* (Horsehair), who eventually turns out to be Óðinn. A venerable adviser, such as Merlin who assists the young Arthur in fulfilling his quests, is an invaluable help. Yet an adviser who can unlock any puzzle is inconvenient if there is to be any achievement in the hero's success, so Gandalf, like Merlin, must be absent for a large part of the tale.

Gandalf appears to have been one of the more powerful of his kind, and was able to vie with Sauron for Frodo's attention when he climbed Amon Hen. He was also able to match the Nazgûl and overcome the Balrog in the depths of Moria, although the encounter killed his physical form. On his return as Gandalf the White, his supremacy is evident. Gandalf wore Narya, the Elvish Ring of Fire, which gave him mastery of that element.

At Frodo's bedside in Rivendell, Gandalf reveals that he was for a while held captive, which surprises Frodo as he had thought his friend a match for any foe, but Gandalf reminds him that there are many powers in the world, some greater than he and others he has never been pitted against. These are prophetic words, since he will later meet a creature which proves his match – the Balrog - and will face other terrors.

The name *Gandalf* occurs in the Old Norse poem *Dvergatal* 'tally of the Dwarves' where it is the name of one of the notable Dwarves of Norse mythology. It is a compound of *gandr* 'magic wand, staff, rod' and *alfr* 'Elf'. The staff of Gandalf plays an important part in the tale, especially in the rousing of King Theoden.

---

[1] Oðinn (Odin) was the Scandinavian god of magic, death and warfare. He was the patron of many Viking leaders. The English knew the god centuries before, under the name Woden. He gave his name to the fourth day of the week: *Wodnesdæg* 'Wednesday'.

Gimli

Gimli (a Dwarf and son of Gloin) went to Rivendell with his father to attend the Council of Elrond. He was chosen to be a member of the Fellowship and to represent his race among the free peoples. Despite the Dwarves' mistrust of the Elves, he became infatuated with Galadriel (an Elf) and this change of heart endeared him to Legolas, the Elf in the Fellowship, so that they became firm friends afterwards. Gimli was present at the Battle of Helm's Deep, and followed Aragorn on the Paths of the Dead although he was terrified by the experience. He rescued Pippin from beneath a dead troll at the Battle of Cormallen Field. After the War of the Ring, he founded a colony of Dwarves in the caves behind Helm's Deep, helped repair Gondor and finally passed into the West with Legolas.

The source for the name Gimli is apparently the Norse *Gimlé* 'lee of fire, place sheltered against flames' – the home of the Light-Elves which would endure the destruction of the world, in the *Prose Edda*.

Glittering Caves

At Helm's Deep, Gimli finds a great wonder – in the caves at the back of the fortress are vast, wondrous caverns where streams run and the walls glisten with veins of ore. The Dwarf describes the sight of the caves with awe and love. Legolas promises to visit the caves with Gimli if they both survive the troubles, if he in turn will one day come to Fangorn.

The Glittering Caves behind Helm's Deep are an unexpected boon to Gimli. He does not descend there to confront fear or danger (the 'descent into the dark' theme), but both are present outside at the battle for the Hornburg. The knowledge of the Caves is the prize won: Gimli later founds a new settlement of his folk there.

Glorfindel

Perhaps more than any other male Elf in *The Lord of the Rings*, Glorfindel embodies the aspect of the Elf as a semi-divine being, imbued with god-like power and majesty. Astride his snow-white horse Asfaloth, he cuts a dashing, resplendent figure. Frodo sees him with a radiance all round him. This may be a reflection of the various sun-gods of northern Europe such as Baldur the Bright in Norse myth or the Irish Lug, all of whom likewise give off an inner light.

Gods – English and Scandanavian

The evidence for the gods of the ancient English is neither as full nor as illuminating as the corresponding Scandinavian material, but the two traditions must originally have been very similar indeed due to their common origins in the Iron Age in Northern Europe. (Christianity came to England in the late 500s from Iona and Augustine's mission from Rome landed in Kent in 597; Scandinavia was largely untouched by the faith for another three centuries, and remained unconverted until the tenth century. The most complete account of Scandinavian mythology comes from the writings of a thirteenth century Icelander, Snorri Sturluson, drawing on already ancient traditions.)

The following are some of the deities worshipped by the English before conversion:

Woden, chief of the gods, is associated with healing and magic, death and the underworld, warfare. He was the favourite of the chiefs and leaders in English society. One OE poem alludes to his fight with the venomous serpent – a myth known from other cultures. His Norse counterpart is Oðinn (Odin). Wednesday (*Wodnesdæg*) is named after this god, as are Wednesbury (*Wodnes burh*, 'Woden's stronghold') and Wansdyke (*Wodnes dic* 'Woden's dyke').

Grim is a by-name of Woden, meaning the 'masked one' referring to the god's habit of travelling in disguise. Some earthworks in East Anglia are named for him: Grim's Dyke.

Thunor (*Þunor*) is the weather-god and protector of men and livestock. His name is the word for 'thunder' (þunor) and he appears to have been associated with fertility, fire and cremation. The Norse equivalent is Þorr (Thor). Thursday (*Þunresdæg*) is named after him, as are Thundersley (*þunres leah*, 'Thunor's glade') and Thunderfield (*þunres feld* 'Thunor's open land').

Tiw is the law-giver and upholder of order; he wages war on the forces of chaos. His name is represented by the rune ↑ which occurs on some Anglo-Saxon swords. One verse of the *OE Rune Poem* refers to the god in terms which suggest a constellation. In Scandinavian tradition, he is called Tyr and is associated with the tale of the binding of the giant wolf, Fenrir. Tuesday (*Tiwesdæg*) and Tysoe (*Tiwes ieg* 'Tiw's island) are named for this god.

Frea is the lord of peace and plenty, good harvests and healthy kin. His sister Frige presides over childbirth and human love. They correspond to the Scandinavian pair Freyr and Freyja. Fryup and Freefolk are English villages named after Frige, as is Friday (*frigedæg*).

Other divine or semi-divine beings lurk in the margins of the historical records. One such is the smith Welund, whose forge stands on the Berkshire Downs. Others occur as names in royal genealogies – figures such as Ash (Æsc), Hengest and Saxnot. The Norse Baldur has an English equivalent in the word *bealdor* 'bold warrior', while Fornet (Norse Fornjotr) has a plant named after him.

The Norse myths recorded by Snorri include a full account of the creation of the world, the exploits of the gods and goddesses and the final destruction through fire and flood.

Gollum - Sméagol

The hobbit Déagol found the Ring in the River Anduin and was murdered for it by his companion Sméagol. The Ring quickly did its work – or was Sméagol already disposed to theft, trickery and deceit? – and the hapless hobbit became the unwitting slave of his 'precious' possession. However, he had too great a resistance to the Ring's power to become a wraith and surrender his will to that of its maker, so the Ring prolonged his life until the opportunity arose for it to further its ends by leaving him.

Having used the power of the Ring to snoop, Sméagol was exiled from his folk. Turning his back on the sun – whose reproving gaze is his conscience – he entered the caves beneath the Misty Mountains, thereby keeping the secret of the Ring's discovery, even its continued existence. Over the long years of his isolation, Sméagol lost most of his identity to the Ring and became the despised creature Gollum; yet a tiny part of his former self remained, enough to enjoy the brief company of a fellow creature, enough to resent his wretched state, enough to hate the Ring he craved. The Ring abandoned Gollum once it had no further use for him, but Gollum could never adjust to life without it. The loss of the Ring induced Gollum to leave his underground home and track first Bilbo then Frodo.

The tale of Gollum is a curious one: far from being just the dark and menacing stalker he at first appears, Gollum gradually becomes a pathetic and pitiable character, if never a likeable one.

Sméagol is an Old English word meaning 'burrowing, delving' based on the same verbal root (**smeug-*) as the name of the dragon Smaug in *The Hobbit*. He was even then obsessed with the origins, roots and causes of things and was always digging in the earth and diving in the water to find secrets. Déagol is likewise Old English and can mean (i) 'secret, hidden, deep', or (ii) 'a hidden place', even 'a grave'. No wonder Tolkien had him meet an untimely end at the hands of Sméagol the Delver.

There is no close analogue of Gollum in any of the northern myths, and his name presumably represents the gulping sound he makes when distressed. Attempts to link it to the *golem*, a vengeful spirit of clay in Hebrew tradition, have not been successful. Gollum perhaps most resembles the Dwarf Andvari in the Norse tale of the cursed ring. Andvari is a malicious hoarder who owns a magical ring, and curses whoever may subsequently wear it after it is taken from him by the gods. In Wagner's opera *Der Ring*, the corresponding character is Alberich. There are other characters in folklore – sometimes heroes or adventurers – who possess magical rings, conferring various powers. The cap or cloak of invisibility is also a fairly widespread narrative device, often worn by a malevolent or predatory creature.

Gondor

See *Dúnedain; Minas Tirith; Mundburg*

Gondor was once ruled by Isildur, the Dúnedain king who destroyed Sauron's army and cut the Ring from his hand. The rulers of Gondor had long been opponents of Sauron and his allies. This had given rise to many invasions and the occupation of its territory. Its central city was captured by Ring Wraiths and held for over a thousand years.

Grima Wormtongue

Grima, a man of Rohan, known to his countrymen as "Wormtongue" is the chief counsellor to King Theoden of the Mark. At some point, he was deceived or bribed into the service of Saruman and began advising the king against involvement in the affairs of other folk. When Gandalf unmasked his treachery, Grima fled to Saruman's tower in Isengard. After the fall of Isengard the two led a miserable existence in the ruins of Saruman's power. Grima's life ends in the Shire where, after killing Saruman, he falls to the arrows of hobbit archers.

Grima is Old English for 'mask, disguise', an appropriate name for an officer of the king who secretly works for his foe.

Halifirien

On the journey from Edoras to Gondor, Pippin and Gandalf pass the various watchtowers which are Gondor's outer defences. The one on the border of Rohan is called *The Halifirien* i.e. Old English *halig firgen* 'holy mountain'. This is one of the few overt references to religion in the book.

Harfoots

See *Hobbits*

Harrowdale

See *Dunharrow*

Harrowdale is the narrow gorge which the Rohirrim pass through on the mountain path from Isengard to Edoras. The road up Harrowdale, to the fortress Dunharrow, winds across the cliff and at each corner there is a statue of a squatting man. These are known as the *Pukel-men* and are very old, so that on some the detail has been lost to erosion.

Dale is a standard English word for 'valley' but the *harrow* element is quite rare. It refers to a heathen temple (OE *hearh*), which usually took the form of an area of cleared ground for assembly within which was one or more idols. These were often wooden posts carved into the likeness of a man or woman, representing the deity. Many such posts were probably decorated with neck-rings, armbands and other jewellery. Like *Halifirien* above, this is a rare religious term brought into Tolkien's work.

Heathen Kings

As the battle rages on Pelennor Field, Denethor says that his son Faramir is burning with fever and now will burn in the flesh, because the West has failed and must end in fire. He says that it is better to burn now than later if the end is unavoidable. Denethor determines to bring about his own death – to lay upon his funeral pyre like the heathen kings of old and pass into death with his son.

The reference to 'heathen kings' is one of the few lapses into modern thought here: being 'post-heathen', Denethor's society is in the position of being Christian. Cremation was a genuine funerary rite of the Angles, contrasted with the inhumation of other Germanic groups, and of Christian tradition.

The rite of cremation was practiced in many areas of early England, mainly on the eastern seaboard in regions associated with the Angles. The dead person's ashes and some long bones were then placed in a decorated pot and buried in a holy place with others. The notion may have been that the spirit of the dead travelled through fire to the Otherworld. Some cemeteries feature both cremation and inhumation, suggesting that the communities using them had mixed religious beliefs and customs.

Helm's Deep

At the end of a valley in the White Mountains, a deep gorge was fortified in ancient times by Helm Hammerhand, a ruler of Rohan. Across the gorge in a narrow place there is a wall of rock called Helm's Gate, and on it a mighty tower called the Hornburg where a trumpet could be blown to resound in the caverns behind. The wall is pierced only by a culvert to allow the Deeping Stream to escape. Erkenbrand, the local commander, had repaired and strengthened the fortifications and made the Hornburg his residence.

King Theoden went to Helm's Deep to resist the forces of Saruman. Here Tolkien uses one of his favourite set-pieces – the motif of the cock-crow being answered by a horn-blast and new hope springing from despair. With the rising sun came Gandalf, the White Rider, and re-enforcements.

Heroic Ideal

Gandalf assures Frodo that what saved him from the Nazgul on Weathertop was 'fortune and fate ... not to mention courage': the fact that Frodo resisted the Nazgûl both physically – he presented a moving target to the attacker – and emotionally – he counter-attacked rather than cowering before the Rider – saved him. The doctrine of resistance to the last is a commonplace of Old English heroic literature. Perhaps its finest expression is in the Old English poem, preserved only as a fragment, called *The Battle of Maldon*.

> It was a hard encounter there. They stood fast,
> those warriors in the strife. Fighting men fell
> weary from their wounds. Gore fell to the ground.
> All the while Oswold and Eadwold
> – both those brothers – encouraged the fighting men,
> bade in their speech their beloved kinsmen
> that they must hold out in their time of need there,
> use their weapons without weakening.
> Byrhtwold spoke up, he raised his shield
> and brandished his spear – he was an old retainer;
> with great courage he addressed the troop:

> "Mind shall be the harder, heart the keener,
> courage the greater as our strength dwindles.
> Here lies our leader, cut down,
> the good man in the dirt. May he ever grieve
> who now thinks to turn from this war-play.
> I am old in life: I do not wish to leave,
> but rather beside my lord,
> – beside so dear a man – do I think to lie."
> Likewise they were encouraged by Æþelgar's son
> Godric, onward to the struggle. Often he sent a spear,
> a slaughter-shaft, spinning into the vikings;
> thus he led the fighting in the battle,
> hewed and slew, till he fell in the fight.
>
> *The Battle of Maldon* – lines 304-324

Hobbits

Tolkien's entire non-academic opus rests on this one curious word 'hobbit'- the quest to understand it led him to create the world of *The Hobbit* and subsequently that of *The Lord of the Rings* and *The Silmarillion.* He later rationalised the word *hobbit* as a derivative of Old English *hol-bytla* 'hole-dweller' (the first thing we learn about the hobbit is that he lived in a hole) although in fact the word already existed as a rare dialect term for 'goblin' or 'brownie'. The race was divided into three groups – Harefoots, Stoors, and Fallohides.

The Harfoots, were darker, shorter, smaller and lived in the uplands. The name may recall Old English *har* 'hoary, grey' or it might be a corruption of *hardfot* 'hard-foot'.

The Stoors were heavier, sturdier and preferred to live on river-plains; their name is based on Old English *stur* 'sturdy'.

The Fallohides were taller and fairer, and lived in woodlands; their name is based on OE *fealu* and *hid* 'yellowish, pale' and 'hide, skin'.

The first hobbit-leaders are Marcho and Blanco, who crossed the River Baranduin with permission of the king. These two clearly recall the legendary earliest English. Their names are based in Old English – *mearh* 'horse' and *blonca* 'white horse'; the reference is to the leaders Hengest 'stallion' and Horsa 'horse?' who arrived in and took control of the south-east of Britain with permission of the post-Roman magnate Vortigern. The nominal leader of the hobbits was called the Thain, the Old English *þegn* 'king's man, retainer, knight'. The land was called the Shire, Old English *scir* 'division, area of land under one leader'; its political congregation the Shiremoot (*scir gemot* 'shire meeting') and its internal executive the Sherriffs (*scir gerefa* 'shire-reeve'). Hobbit dwellings of the underground type were called *smials*, which is (like *Smaug*) a derivative of the verb **smeugan* 'delve, crawl inside'.

Tolkien devised the word "mathomhouse" to describe what we would call a "museum" or "antiquarian collection. The concept of a museum – in this case, of the Victorian kind, a collection of curiosities and antiquities – was unknown before the modern age, but the early English certainly knew the word *maþþum* for an object of mainly sentimental and prestige value (Tolkien's 'mathom'). An assemblage of such items might well be kept in a Mathom-house.

Hobbits are representative of the English countryfolk of Tolkien's youth, with their insatiable appetites for beer, plentiful food and tobacco. While apparently dour, they were keen on singing, dancing, games and pastimes. They were simple folk by choice, eschewing education in favour of learning. They enjoyed word-games, gifts and hospitality, as the Anglo-Saxons are known to have done. Their lifestyle was founded on the twin principles of comfort and respectability, ones familiar to suburban people today. But while they were self-indulgent they were also self-sufficient: frequent meals are only possible through hard work.

The internal divisions of the Shire – the four Farthings – are pure Old English; 'farthing' is *feorþing* 'fourth part, quarter'; the Marches are *mearcas* 'borderlands' and Buckland is Old English *bocland* 'land granted by charter'. The ruined and legendary royal governmental centre at far-off Fornost had dwindled to the comfortable Kings' Norbury (*norþ burh* 'northern fortress').

Hobbits are depicted in familiar human terms – indeed, they come off the page as much more like real people than some of the humans do. The idea that the unimportant, small, comfort-loving folk of an obscure corner of the world could have more profound moral fortitude than the great and the good seems incongruous at first; it stems from Tolkien's appreciation of the stubborn courage of the 'other ranks', the troops who endured so much in the trenches of the Great War. The tale of the acceptance and execution of an impossible task by the lowly and despised, while their alleged betters founder, is deeply satisfying on one level.

In *The Lord of the Rings* hobbits act as the lens through which most scenes are viewed and to a large extent hobbits represent the modern reader in the tale: they feel out-of-place, powerless and lost among the momentous and frightening events taking place around them. Like the reader, the hobbits have to make sense of new names and ideas; again like the reader, the hobbits gradually grow in stature and strength from undertaking the perilous task.

Hollin

The region to the west of the mines of Moria is called, in the Common Speech, *Hollin*. Its symbol is the holly tree. In Elvish it was called *Eregion*.

The name *Hollin* is the normal development of Old English *holegn* 'holly'. Holly was one of the noble trees of mediaeval legend, as mentioned in the traditional carol *The Holly and the Ivy*: "of all the trees that are in the wood, the holly bears the crown." Its evergreen leaves were a symbol of everlasting life, and may have been so in pre-Christian times.

Horn-Blast and Cock-Crow

After the gates of Minas Tirith have been battered down, only the White Rider (Gandalf) bars the way to the Black Rider (Ringwraith). As they confront each other, far off in the city a cock crows to greet the morning. As if in answer, the sound of horns is heard approaching from the north: Rohan has come.

Here – and in several other places in the story - Tolkien uses the motif of a horn blast as a gesture of defiance towards the foe but opposes it to the cock-crow signalling morning – the passage of night into day, as also the passage from dark despair to bright hope.

Isengard

Isengard lies in a naturally defended place with high rock walls thrust out from the mountain, which have been supplemented by a wall of impregnable stonework and heavy gates. Saruman had already turned it from a pleasant garden to a huge industrial complex with open mineshafts, workshops and furnaces ranged around the interior. In the centre stands the wizard's black tower, Orthanc.

The name is OE *isen geard* 'iron yard', a place where metalworking takes place. It describes the huge complex of industrial and ore-mining sites which Saruman constructs around his tower, Orthanc.

Isildur

Isildur, the chief of the Men of the West, defeated Sauron's army and cut the Ring from his hand with his father's sword, which caused it to shatter. Isildur failed to summon the will to destroy the Ruling Ring when he had the chance. Several years later, while attempting to escape from Orcs, he put on the Ring to make himself invisible. As he swam across a river, the Ring slipped from his finger and he was killed.

The Ring betrayed Isildur to his death, but the shards of his sword, *Narsil* 'white fire', were brought to Rivendell, where they remained waiting their re-forging. The sword is eventually wielded in the War of the Ring by Aragorn, Isildur's heir, re-named *Anduril* 'Flame of the West'

Isildur's Bane

A name for the Ruling Ring, which serves to remind one and all that the Ring will never serve its possessor but seek always to return to the hand of the Dark Lord who made it. (Bane – OE *bana*, something that causes death or destruction.)

Journey into the West

In a final 'escape from death', Frodo and Sam pass west over the sundering sea to the Undying Lands, with the last bearers of the Elven Rings. Although they explicitly were not dead, they were nevertheless irreversibly parted from their homes and families – unless any should later join them. In this sense, the journey into the west is akin to the heathen tradition of ship-burial whereby the dead are thought to continue their lives on the far shore. There could be no return for Frodo, any more than there could for the East Anglian king in Mound 1 at Sutton Hoo.

King of the Dead

See *Ringwraiths*

As the narrow pass from the end of the Paths of the Dead broadens into a lush valley, Aragorn urges his followers to ride quickly. The houses of the valley-dwellers are shut and darkened against them as they ride swiftly through the night, believing that the King of the Dead has returned.

This motif is an echo of the Wild Hunt of English folklore in which a troop of ghostly riders wreak havoc across the countryside, often led by a figure from local folklore. Leaders include Sir Francis Drake and Robin Hood, but the original King of the Dead was the god Woden who led the souls of the unquiet dead across the night sky in a cavalcade of terror.

Lathspell

"Lathspell" is the byname Grima uses of Gandalf when the wizard visits Edoras to rouse King Theoden against Saruman. He accuses Gandalf of always bringing bad news and trouble with him – implying that he is either himself a troublemaker, or that he only visits Rohan when he needs its help.

"Lathspell" is OE, formed from the words *lað* 'hateful, inimical, loathsome' and *spell* 'speech, story, message' – the meaning is approximately 'troublesome tidings' or 'bad news'. The religious point underlying this name is that it must be contrasted with its Old English antonym *godspell* 'good news' from which the word 'gospel' derives. Theologically, the 'good news' is Greek *euaggelion*, evangelium, the word of God.

Legolas

Legolas is a Sindarin or Grey-Elf who journeyed to Rivendell to take part in the Council of Elrond. He was chosen to accompany Frodo in the Fellowship. Despite the traditional antipathy between Elves and Dwarves, the devotion of Gimli (a Dwarf) to Galadriel touched him greatly and the two became firm friends. In the pursuit of the Orcs across the Plain of Rohan, Legolas's keen sight was a great help to Aragorn. He took part in the Battle of Helm's Deep, accompanied Aragorn on the Paths of the Dead, and arrived with him at the Battle of Pelennor Fields. Galadriel warned him that the sight of the sea would cause him great distress, and so it proved as he was never at home in the woods after that. He passed into the West with his friend Gimli after the death of Aragorn.

Lothlorien

Lothlorien ("golden flower") is a sylvan paradise, a deep wood so powerful, so charged with Elvish spirituality, that it actively repels the unworthy. It is a beautiful image, which has captured the imagination of many. Due to the potency of its keeper, Galadriel, it exists in a kind of time-warp whereby the passage of time within the heart of the wood is slower than in the profane world outside.

"Man in the Moon"

The 'Man in the Moon' song performed by Frodo at Bree is of course an extended version of the popular nursery rhyme. Tolkien considered areas such as folklore, local legends, songs and rhymes to be the last hiding places of a whole body of myth and legend which – like tatty furniture - had been consigned to the nursery before being thrown out for good. One example is the use of 'she' for the sun – normal among Elves and hobbits, but also the prevailing view in Old English and Old Norse (*seo sunne* is a feminine noun in Old English).

Mearas

The Mearas were beautiful, silvery-white wild horses first tamed by the Rohirrim. King Eorl's horse was called Felarof, an Old English word with the meaning 'famed for many deeds'. *Mearas* is itself one of many Old English terms meaning 'horses'. The Mearas would only allow members of the royal line of Rohan to ride them, except for Shadowfax who was to bear Gandalf on his adventures.

The name *Shadowfax* 'shadow-mane' is based on the divine horses of Norse tradition: *Hrímfaxi* 'dewy-mane' and *Skinfaxi* 'shining-mane', who pulled the chariots of the moon and sun respectively.

English warriors in the pagan period generally did not fight on horseback, although they did ride to war and used their horses in hunting. Some were buried with their mounts: two such burials were found at Lakenheath, Suffolk, and in Mound 17 at Sutton Hoo.

The notion of the taboo horse is not unique. It is said by Bede that priests of the English heathen religion were not allowed to carry weapons or ride a stallion. There is also a late Icelandic tradition, in *Hrafnkels Saga*, that the priest of Freyr owned a horse which none but he might ride: when a servant disobeyed and mounted the horse, Hrafnkel was bound by the terms of his oath to kill him. In the *Germania*, Tacitus mentions the prophetic powers of Germanic horses and the duty of kings to interpret their neighing.

The following are the names of the Mearas with their standard Old English equivalents and meanings:

Arod	*arod*	swift, fast
Felarof	*felarof*	much-famed
Hasufel	*hasu, fell*	grey + coat
Windfola	*wind, fola*	wind + foal

Compare the name of the pony Meriadoc rode in Rohan – Stybba 'stumpy', from Old English *stybb* 'tree-stump'.

Meduseld

See also *Edoras*

Meduseld is the royal hall of King Theoden of the Mark, the 'King of the Golden Hall'. It is one of the most evocative words in Old English tradition: it means 'mead-hall' and conjures up visions of communal feasting, good food and drink, friendship, security and warmth. It was the highest expression of all that was good and desirable in early English life.

The golden decorations and fittings of Meduseld echo the splendour of the hall *Heorot* in *Beowulf* where King Hroþgar of the Danes ordered to be built the greatest of meadhalls ever heard of.

Melted Sword

After the fight with the Black Captain, Merry is left alone to gather his shield and sword; the blade has melted at the blow to the Nazgûl. It was a blade of Westernesse, taken from the Barrowdowns, and its power against the Nazgûl was great, as its maker had forged it in the wars against Angmar.

As with the sword used in the attack at Weathertop, the melting of the blade after it has despatched the supernatural foe is drawn from the similar incident in *Beowulf* where, having slain Grendel's Mother, the mighty sword dissolves in her hot blood before the hero's gaze.

Men & Ghosts of Men

All the various races of men share a common inheritance and origin, and all share a common future. One of Tolkien's strokes of genius was to set *The Lord of the Rings* at the very point where the Ents, Elves, Dwarves and other sentient creatures are finally pushed into the background as the Age of Men dawns in Middle-Earth. By implication, this is the very time when the tales of the various non-humans begin the transition from history to legend to folktale. Here the myths of later ages were created.

There are three degrees or kinds of Men. The High Men are descended from the Númenorians; their only representatives are the Dúnedain, the Men of the

West. The Middle Men, or Men of the Twilight, include the Rohirrim, the men of Bree and the other rustic and semi-civilised men of Middle-Earth. The third degree includes the Wild Men or Men of Darkness, such as the Easterlings, the Southrons, the Dunlendings and the Woses.

A unique group are those men whose ghosts inhabit the Paths of the Dead. Here, Tolkien drew on the Germanic tradition of oath-taking as the most solemn and serious of human activities. These men had sworn loyalty to Isildur, but refused the call to arms against Sauron. Isildur cursed them to remain after death until his heir should summon them to fulfil their oath of loyalty. There is also more than a little of the *Einherjar* in these ghosts: these are the champions of Óðinn who had followed his cult in life and were privileged to follow their god after death, until the final battle in which the world would perish. The notion that an oath could bind a man beyond death is ancient in northern tradition.

Perhaps related are the ghosts of Men, Elves and Orcs in the Dead Marshes who wait to lure unwary travellers down to their death in the rank waters of the marsh. The tradition recalls the will-o'-the-wisp – a spirit with a lighted wisp of straw who encouraged people crossing marshes to follow him, only to lead them to their doom. (The physical effect is the ignition of methane – marsh gas – resulting in brief bursts of flame, which travellers might try to follow.)

Merry

Meriadoc Brandybuck, known as "Merry" was a close friend of Frodo's and saw through the latter's attempts to disguise his plan to leave the Shire. At the Council of Elrond, Merry was chosen to be in the Fellowship of the Ring. His capture by Orcs with his friend Pippin led to the rousing of the Ents and the downfall of Saruman. Later, he dealt one of the blows which destroyed the Black Captain of the Nazgûl, though he nearly paid for this with his life. On his return to the Shire he organised the overthrow of the Saruman administration, and was later made Master of Buckland.

Meriadoc or Meriadec was the name of a 6th century Welsh saint who sold off his landholdings and gave them to the poor. His name means 'sea guardian'.

Midday Gloom

During the preparation of the defences at Minas Tirith, the great gloom out of the east casts a pall over the whole sky and obliterates the sunrise. This leaves the Men of Gondor feeling uneasy and dejected.

The permanent gloom which is caused by the fumes and smokes of Mordor being pumped high into the atmosphere recalls the Norse concept of *fimbulvetr* "Great Winter", a period of permanent cold and dark lasting three years with no summers between. It is one of the tokens by which men will know that the Fall of the Gods is approaching.

Middle Earth

This is the name Tolkien gave to the fictional 'world' of his tales. It is not presented as fictional, but as northern and western Europe ("the North-West of the Old World, east of the Sea") in a remote period of post-glacial prehistory. In common with ancient Europe, it is conceived as marching with an extensive landmass to the east and an ocean to the west. It resembles its namesake, the *middangeard* 'middle-enclosure' of Anglo-Saxon tradition, the part of the world which men inhabit. *Middangeard* was surrounded by the realms of Elves and Dwarves, with *heofon* (heaven, home of the gods) above and *hel* (hell, home of the dead) below. It was in the middle of a set of localities.

Middle-Earth is a continent of mountains, forests, rolling plains and marshy bogs, moorland, lakes and fields. It is, in effect, much like northern and western Europe after the coming of men (c. 50,00 years ago) but before the processes of mechanisation and industrialisation took hold over men's hearts (c.300 years ago). Tolkien described it tellingly as 'the quiet of the world, when there was less noise and more green'. It contains within it designated areas of ancient enchanted woodland (e.g. Lothlorien, Fangorn) which are in a sense timeless. Indeed the sense of vast time-spans and long histories is strong in *The Lord of the Rings* where traditions may stretch back a millennium or more, unbroken by invasion or suppression. The setting and material culture of the book is generally consistent with the mediaeval period of European history, although the hobbits know such post-mediaeval introduced plants as the tomato, potato and pipeweed (tobacco plant). Much of the social structure and culture of Middle-Earth is feudal or post-Roman at the time of the story, but Tolkien skilfully blends elements from a variety of historic periods to produce a 'vaguely mediaeval' feeling which is nevertheless impossible to pin down to one era. It resembles most the mediaeval treatment of ancient legend, in which the narrative describes the deeds of Bronze or Iron Age heroes, but dresses them up in the armour and weapons of the crusading knights.

The map of Middle-Earth supplied with *The Lord of the Rings* appears to pre-date the story so that the characters move across and through an unknown, inconvenient and sometimes hostile landscape. This sense that Tolkien was more of a map-reader than a map-maker gives the story a realistic grounding – this is less true of *The Hobbit* where geography seems to be secondary to the need to introduce a further adventure at certain points in the narrative.

Minas Tirith

See *Gondor*

In *The Lord of the Rings*, the first city of Gondor is Minas Tirith, which sits on an outcrop of Mount Mindolluin. This fortress city, which is also known as Mundburg, rises in seven terraces above the plain with the topmost level capped by a tall tower called Minas Tirith "Tower of the Guard".

The seven walled terraces of the city of Minas Tirith may reflect the Seven Hills on which Rome was founded. Gondor's relationship to Rohan is similar in many ways to that of Rome to the peoples of Germanic Europe. (The siege of Gondor may even have echoes of the Siege of Constantinople.)

Mithril

During Bilbo Baggin's adventures, as told in *The Hobbit*, he was given a *mithril coat*, a mailshirt made by the Dwarves. It was light as a feather and harder than steel. Bilbo gave it to Frodo, who wore it beneath his outer clothes.

Mithril confers a form of semi-invulnerability on the hobbit, although like all mail it protects against slashing and hacking blows but cannot prevent a concussion injury from the weight of the blow.

Mordor

Mordor is the kingdom of Sauron. It has mountain defences to the North, West, and South. In the north is Mount Doom and Sauron's Dark Tower.

The 'land of Mordor where the shadows lie' is the home and heartland of all that is evil in Middle-Earth. The word is rationalised as Sindarin, meaning 'black land', but it is hardly coincidence that *mordor* is the Old English word for 'murder, unlawful killing'.

The use of 'shadow' in *The Lord of the Rings* is always suggestive: shadows have a palpable force and all evil things in the books make use of darkness (or obscured light) to move around, to inspire fear and to confuse their opponents.

Within the encircling mountains of Mordor, on the plain, there were many camps full of Mordor soldiers: drab rows of huts and low buildings. The troops had been assembled for an attack against the West and were bivouacked around Mount Doom in preparation for the order to move out.

The description of the great plain and the dismal, dreary camps set on it can hardly be based on anything but first-hand experience of the military, probably the rigours of life on campaign in the First World War. The relentless bustle and pointless activity are both associated with campaign life.

Mouth of Sauron

The Army of the West advances on Mordor after the Battle of Pelennor Fields and a small group of heralds is despatched to the gate. A tall black-clad figure, whose name is forgotten, rides out to them: he had earnt Sauron's favour with his cunning and cruelty, and is called the Mouth of Sauron.

The importance of names to personal identity is paramount in many societies, and the knowledge of a person's true name gives one power over the person. The fact that the Mouth of Sauron has no name of his own indicates strongly that he has been subjugated totally to the will and personality of the Dark Lord.

Mundburg

See *Minas Tirith* and *Gondor*

The name *Mundburg* is OE 'protecting fortress', a descriptive name for the last bastion of the West. It is what the Riders of Rohan call Minas Tirith.

The Gondorian gate-guards' direct manner of speech echoes the first challenge received by Beowulf on his journey to meet king Hroþgar of the Danes. Beowulf is advised to declare his name and lineage and state his business lest he be considered a *leasesceawere*, a 'dishonest looker' or 'spy'.

Mysterious Wayfarer

Camping overnight in Fangorn Forest, Gimli sees a figure on the edge of the firelight, wrapped in a great cloak, with a broad-brimmed hat, leaning on his staff. Aragorn offers the stranger a place at their fire, but he soon discovers that the mysterious visitor has gone, and so have their horses.

The description of the traveller is based on the Norse version of the god Woden (Óðinn), travelling in his guise of a footweary old man. The large slouch hat is pulled down to hide the god's empty eye socket.

Narsil

See *Isildur*

Narya

Narya - the Elvish Ring of Fire. It was worn by Gandalf and gave him mastery of that element.

Nazgûl

see *Ringwraiths*

Númenor

This is a sunken land in the Western Seas – an Atlantis in Middle-Earth – and its people are the most gifted and longest-lived of men. Their descendants, the men of Gondor, have inherited a reduced form of these traits. With Eressëa, the Lonely Isle, it forms the area Eldamar or Elvenhome, since Elves inhabit both regions. To the west of Númenor lies Valinor, the realm of the Valar.

Númenor is in the Undying Lands in the west, which are the source of all civilisation in Middle-Earth, a retort to the Victorian notion of *ex orient lux* (light from the East) which regarded the Near East as the origin of all human progress.

The lands in the west, beyond the setting sun, feature large in the folklore and mythology of many Atlantic European peoples. There are many traditions of heroes passing into the west, among which the best-known is Arthur who, in some accounts, was taken at the point of death in a boat over the waters to the 'land of Avalon'. The name *Avalon* is based on the same root as our word 'apple' and means 'the land of orchards', a place of undying plenty. There is a close mythic association between immortality and apples, as for example the Norse goddess Idunn who keeps a crock of the fruit for the gods to eat so that they may retain their youth and vigour. The Garden of the Hesperides, where Herakles found the apples of gold, is another example of this idea. The Irish refer to the lands in the west as *Tir na nOg* 'land of youth'. The underlying idea is that the sun sets (dies) in the west yet manages to re-appear at dawn in the east – therefore there must be some special place in the far west where renewal and revival takes place. There is thus a thematic association between the west, death and rebirth.

Legends of lost cities or whole kingdoms sunk beneath the waves are common in coastal districts. In some cases, ancient fish-traps made of hurdles have been re-interpreted as the foundations of houses. Yet not all such tales are mythic: a whole Anglo-Saxon cathedral city, called Dunwich, has been lost to the sea. It stood on the shore of East Anglia, not far from Walton Castle – a Roman coastal fort which is now nearly a mile out to sea.

Oath-Breaking

See *Paths of the Dead*

The Dead whom Aragorn summons to fulfil their vow are the ghosts of oath-breakers from centuries before.

The notion of an oathbreaker being condemned to continual posthumous torment is drawn from Norse mythology, where Hel – the realm of punishment – is populated with adulterers, cowards and oathbreakers. In fact, all three groups share the characteristic of failing to fulfil their obligations – spouses who break the wedding vow, warriors who break the vow of military service and dishonest men who swear false oaths.

The Rohirrim have a tale of an ancient leader called Baldor who foolishly went off in fulfilment of a vow to pass through the Paths of the Dead, and it is implied that Baldor's remains are the skeleton seen by the Dunedain at the doorway on the Path.

The theme of the foolish vow is picked up from *Beowulf* where King Hroðgar's adviser, Hunferþ, accuses the hero of having recklessly risked his life in a swimming match with another man.

Old Man Willow and the Old Forest

See *Tom Bombadil* and *Withywindle*

Frodo, Sam, Merry and Pippin, travelling out of the Shire through the Old Forest, come upon a willow-choked river. As they walk on they find themselves becoming drowsier with every step and eventually fall asleep against a huge willow tree. Frodo manages to resist the soporific spell of the tree and Sam is wary enough to feel the drowsiness is unnatural. Frodo begins calling for help and a strange figure in bright clothing emerges from the wood; he names himself Tom Bombadil and straightaway sings over the tree to release the captives.

The murky forest is an ancient theme of myth, the scene of awesome initiations and the home of unspoken fears. The primeval forest – hostile to man, lair of dangerous and unseen creatures – is also a feature of many ancient tales. The seductive and murderous Old Man Willow is a reminder that the natural world is no mere passive resource for man to exploit, but a potent ecosystem comprising many orders of being.

Oliphaunt

Frodo and Sam watch as Faramir sets an ambush for southerners who are joining Sauron's army. When the fighting starts the hobbits are alarmed by the bellowing roar of an *oliphaunt* as it crashes out of the trees and lurches past their hiding place. Sam is shocked but delighted at having seen the legendary beast.

An *oliphaunt* is a huge beast capable of carrying a fortification on its back. The description fits well an Indian *howdah* mounted on an oversized elephant-like creature.

Orcs

Orcs are a race of Goblins who seek pleasure in destruction, cruelty, inspiring fear and inflicting pain on others. They are hideous, swarthy creatures with long, strong ape like arms. Their blood flows black and cold. They are fierce fighters and the servants of the Dark Lord. They have good night eyes but fear light.

The word *Orc* meaning 'goblin' is not recorded in Old English but the *Beowulf* poet certainly knew the expression *orcneas* 'Orc-corpses' (perhaps the undead?) as one of a series of evil supernatural creatures which were among the kindred of Cain. There is another (Latin) word *orcus* meaning a god of the underworld, which gave rise to the French (and later English) word 'ogre'; Tolkien may have had this in mind in choosing a name for the race of bloodthirsty, destructive, carnivorous brutes. That said, the hybrid *Uruk-hai* bred by Saruman in his Genetic Modification experiments had some near-human qualities: courage, loyalty and a fierce resilience.

Tolkien's hatred of wanton destruction, casual cruelty, mindless defacement is a theme throughout his works. The treatment of the statue of the noble king at the crossroads in Ithilien is symbolic of their work: it is hacked about, and smeared with graffiti, and its head has been knocked off and left in the undergrowth, replaced by a crude stone with a red eye daubed on it. The statue's head lies at the roadside, now covered with creepers which give the impression of a living crown draped around it. Frodo takes heart from this affirmation of the power of nature.

Tolkien loathed the uprooting and killing of trees through industrialization in his own day; we need not doubt that he would have reacted even more strongly to the graffiti, despair, litter and mindless destruction of the post-industrial society. The despised Orcs cannot make anything for themselves – nothing of worth or beauty, anyway – yet they are quite willing to smash and spoil any good thing they find, for no reason other than that they can.

Orthanc

In the centre of Isengard stands Orthanc, a black tower made from four pillars joined into one pinnacle. Saruman's alterations to the original design make the tower more resemble the tower of the Dark Lord.

Orthanc is the tower which Saruman inhabits. Its name is analysed as Sindarin 'Mount Fang' but is also the Old English word (*orþanc*) for 'cleverness, cunning, especially mechanical skill'. Saruman's special delight is the mechanical contraptions which Tolkien so despised, and the destruction and pollution which they cause.

Palantir

The *Palantir* is one of a number of 'seeing-stones' by which the user of any one can communicate with the others. Sauron used his palantir to expose other users to the pernicious influence of his evil. The connection with the crystal ball of mediaeval tradition is obvious. Examples of rock-crystal spheres have been found in Anglo-Saxon graves from south-east England. They are suspected of having symbolic status, but may have been used as magnifying glasses.

The name *Palantir* is explained as "that which looks far away" which is close to what 'telescope' means (Greek *tele* 'far off' *skopein* 'to see') – a humorous calque on the modern invention.

Paths of the Dead

See *Oath Breaking*

From the *palantir* at Isengard, Aragorn learns of a threat to Minas Tirith approaching from the south, and his only hope of intercepting it is to cross the mountains through the Paths of the Dead. This is a fearful place but Aragorn has been reminded of an ancient prophecy about Isildur's heir. The Dead are oathbreakers, men who swore to fight Sauron in the First War but failed to fulfil their promise to Isildur, who cursed them not to rest until their debt is paid. Their ghosts still haunt the mountain pass and for that reason the Men of Rohan fear to go there. Aragorn has no living supporters, other than the few with him now, so calling on the Dead is his last, desperate measure.

This episode is a classic 'descent into the dark' where the fear to be faced is the wraiths of the oathbreakers, the vengeful ghosts of the dead. The prize won by this encounter is the defeat of the attacking fleet of Corsairs, and thus the timely arrival of the Dunedain.

Pippin

"Pippin" is a byname for Peregrine Took, a long time friend of Frodo's. At the Council of Elrond, Pippin was determined to accompany Frodo and Sam. He contributes to the tale through two major errors: rousing the Orcs in Moria and looking into the *Palantir*. Nevertheless, with Merry he roused the Ents from their complacency, swore allegiance to the Steward of Gondor, prevented Denethor from murdering his own son, and took part in the battle before the Black Gate where he was trapped under a dead troll and had to be rescued by Gimli.

The name Peregrin is Latin for 'pilgrim, wayfarer' but Pippin was also the name borne by a powerful Frankish ruler, who was responsible for annexing the territory of the Old Saxons into the Frankish Empire.

Plain of Gorgoroth

The description of the plain of Gorgoroth, running from near the Black Gate to Mount Doom some fifty miles away, as a field of craters with fissures running between them recalls the shell-holes, fighting positions, forward posts and communications trenches of the First World War. The notion that it is possible to creep from hiding place to hiding place unobserved is typical of the concealed troop movements (below the parapet of the trenches) which characterised this phase of military history.

Púkel-Men

See *Woses* and *Dunharrow*

Merry meets Woses in Druadan Forest and follows an escort to the king's tent, where Theoden and Eomer sit facing a squat, gnarled man wearing only a grass kilt; he resembles the images of the Púkel-men on the Dunharrow.

The Púkel-men are a race of human beings from ancient times. They appear to lead a hunter-gatherer existence, of a kind which was replaced by pastoralism some 5,000 years ago across much of Eurasia, and subsequently by settled agriculture. Their monument – the Harrowdale – is unlike anything normally associated with hunter-gatherer societies and would have required enormous organisation and stored resources to complete. Tolkien implies that they are the indigenous inhabitants of Middle-Earth, now disregarded by the more organised societies of that land.

Pucel or the variant *puca* is an Old English term for a goblin or brownie, familiar to modern readers from Shakespeare's *A Midsummer Night's Dream*. It was revived by Kipling in the tale *Puck of Pook's Hill*. Also known as Robin Goodfellow, Puck in mediaeval tradition was a mischievous character who still could be persuaded to help out with domestic chores. Living a parallel existence to human beings, Puck was unconcerned with men's cares and hopes.

Quickbeam

The tree-name *quickbeam*, describing the hastiest of the ent-folk, is another example of Tolkien's word-play: it comes from Old English *cwicbeam* 'living tree' and refers to its supposed quickening (life-bringing) powers.

Radagast

Radagast the Brown is a shadowy figure in *The Lord of the Rings*, appearing only in the report of Gandalf at the Council of Elrond. He is one of only three wizards in the tale. He appears to have special care of animal life, being able to talk with birds and beasts, and to change his shape. It has been suggested that the timely arrival of Gwaihir and the eagles at various points in the tale is due to the intervention of Radagast.

Radagast (or Radegast, Radihost) was a god of the Slavs of Eastern Europe. He was considered to offer good advice, and to be concerned with honour and strength. His name is based on the element *radost* 'joy, gladness, bliss' which may indicate that he, like Óðinn, is a personification of wishing, of the human will. Given that Radagast's associations include conversing with animals and a sense of bliss, it is likely enough that a shamanic element can be detected in his cult.

Rammas Wall

Tolkien had a pointed, satirical note in his description of the wall of Rammas Echor, a breastwork built to defend the west, which proves ultimately useless. It was constructed after Mordor overran Ithilien, to enclose the fertile plain of Pelennor lying east of the city and down near to the River Anduin at Harlond. There are echoes of the French Maginot Line, built after World War I at enormous cost and effort to provide a permanent defence against the Germans; it was quickly outflanked during the German invasion at the start of World War II.

Rangers

The Rangers or Dunedain (Men of the West) are the last remnant of the Men of Numenorean stock in Arnor, the northern kingdom. Landless, they nevertheless use their remarkable gifts in the service of Gandalf and the Elves by holding back the threat to the West of the Orcs of the Misty Mountains and other allies of Sauron. They are expert trackers and scouts. Tolkien seems to have drawn on the many legendary scouts and hunters of the Wild West as much as European tradition for these characters.

Riders of the Mark

The following is a selection of the names from Rohan, with their standard Old English equivalents[1] and meaning (like genuine Old English names, they are often composed from two separate words):

Aldor	*ealdor*	elder, leader
Baldor	*bealdor*	prince, leader
Brego	*brego*	champion, hero
Brytta	*brytta*	distributor (usually of treasure)
Ceorl	*ceorl*	yeoman, freeman
Deor	*deor*	brave, bold, fierce
Deorwine	*deor, wine*	dear + friend
Dernhelm	*dyrne, helm*	secret + helmet
Dunhere	*dun, here*	highland + warband
Elfhelm	*ælf, helm*	Elf + helmet
Elfhild	*ælf, hild*	Elf + battle
Elfwine	*ælf, wine*	Elf + friend
Eomer	*eoh, mære*	horse + famed
Eomund	*eoh, mund*	horse + hand, protector
Eorl	*eorl*	hero, war-leader
Eothain	*eoh, þegn*	horse + retainer, servant
Eowyn	*eoh, wynn*	horse + joy
Erkenbrand	*eorcen, brand*	splendid + flame
Fastred	*fæst, ræd*	firm + advice
Fengel	*fengel*	leader, receiver of treasure
Folca	*folc*	tribal muster, army, people, folk
Folcred	*folc, ræd*	folk + advice
Folcwine	*folc, wine*	folk + friend
Fram	*fram*	effective, purposeful
Frea	*frea*	lord, beloved one
Frealaf	*frea, laf*	lord + survivor
Freawine	*frea, wine*	lord + friend
Frumgar	*frum, gar*	first + spear
Galmod	*galmod*	wanton, destructive
Gamling	*gamol*	aged
Garulf	*gar, wulf*	spear + wolf
Gleowine	*gleo, wine*	song + friend
Goldwine	*gold, wine*	gold + friend
Grima	*grima*	mask, face-plate on helmet, disguise
Grimbold	*grim, bold*	grim + bold
Guthlaf	*guþ, laf*	battle + survivor
Haleth	*hæleð*	hero, warrior
Hama	*hama*	garment, covering
Harding	*heard*	hardy, brave

[1] Tolkien often used Mercian forms, which are slightly different from the standard West Saxon ones.

Helm	*helm*	helmet
Herefara	*here, fara*	army + traveller
Herubrand	*heoru, brand*	sword + flame
Hild	*hild*	battle
Holdwine	*hold, wine*	trustworthy + friend
Horn	*horn*	horn
Leod	*leod*	prince, leader
Leofa	*leofa*	beloved, dear
Thengel	*þengel*	prince, prosperous person
Theoden	*þeoden*	folk-leader, ruler
Theodred	*þeod, ræd*	folk + advice
Theodwyn	*þeod, wynn*	folk + joy
Walda	*wealda*	wielder, ruler
Widfara	*wid, fara*	wide + traveller
Wulf	*wulf*	wolf

Rings of Power –Ruling Ring; Master Ring; One Ring

See *Gollum*

Sauron had the Rings of Power forged by the Elves. He then forged the One Ring – the Master Ring – the Ruling Ring, which made him Lord of the Rings.

Twenty rings were made.

- Three for the Elf-lords, who hid from Sauron and have not been touched by his power.
- Seven for the Dwarf-kings, three of these rings Sauron recovered, and four were devoured by dragons.
- Nine for Mortal Men, all of which ensnared kings and made them Sauron's servants. They are the Black Riders, the Ringwraiths.
- One for the Dark Lord, Sauron. Much of Sauron's power was vested in this Master-ring. If he recovers it he will regain his lost powers and more beside, and rule over all those who have the other rings.

The One Ring was taken from Sauron when Men and Elves fought together against him. During the battle, Isildur hacked the Ring from Sauron's hand. Having gained the Ring, Isildur had the opportunity to destroy it but kept it, only to lose it in a river while fleeing from Orcs. There the Ring lay until a hobbit found it. He was murdered by his companion, who came to be called *Gollum*. From him the Ring passed to Bilbo and then Frodo.

Around the inside of the Ring, in Elvish letters in the Black Speech of Mordor, is written,

One Ring to rule them all, One Ring to find them,
One Ring to bring them all and in the darkness bind them.

The One Ring gives Sauron power over any person or race that possess one of the lesser rings of power. Those mortals who bear the Ring will not die but will eventually grow extremely weary. The Ring will make the wearer invisible but each time it is used he will fade until he remains invisible for all time and become subject to the Dark Lord, Sauron. The Dark Power will devour all who use the Ring, however strong or well intentioned they are.

Sauron's Ruling Ring is the antithesis of all that Tolkien loved. It represents the human love of gold (wealth) and human skill in making simple-looking but powerful machines (industry). The Ring's ability to excite the worst passions in all who behold it is indicative of the insidious nature of technology – that seems to promise so much beauty and power, but actually enslaves the user.

The central notion of *The Lord of the Rings* is that the One Ring forged by Sauron is inherently corrosive to the free will, a part of its master's power and personality. The apt proverb 'all power tends to corrupt, and absolute power corrupts absolutely' was coined in relation to human dictators of various political hues. Tolkien's reflection on the idea takes it a stage further: what if the mesmerising power of an item of treasure were allied to (and derived from) an unyielding, dominating, evil personality?

The notion of rings having special powers is itself quite ancient. The Norse god Óðinn had among his chief treasures a ring Draupnir, from which every ninth night nine further rings would issue – a clear statement that wealth begets wealth. This ring was sent with his favourite son, Baldur, to the world of the dead but was later returned to the god.

Rings were prized above all other treasures by the early English, both finger-rings and arm-rings. They were used in a complex system of service and reward within the military culture of the period. Military service was voluntary, and the best warriors had to be enticed to follow the best leaders by the promise of the best rewards, taking the form of adornments which were prominently displayed. The act of bestowing a ring on a follower was a highly public expression of approval and gratitude. The warriors earnt this bounty with deeds of courage on behalf of their lord, who was known as *beahgifa* 'ring-giver', *sinces brytta* 'distributor of treasure', and so on. The lord's gift of rings was therefore not an act of selfless kindness: many fought bravely to earn renown and bought their rewards at a huge cost of personal injury and death. The true 'Lord of the Rings' was not merely a warm-hearted bestower of bounty, he was also a war-leader and tribal chief.

From this duality within the act of treasure-giving arose the idea that rings were inherently powerful and deceitful. It was a small step from there to seeing a malevolent force inherent in such rings.

Ringwraiths

The Ringwraiths or Black Riders are the Nazgûl, the zombie-like souls of nine human kings who are unable to die while they are subservient to the One Ring. Their leader, the Witch-King of Angmar, was the subject of a prophecy: that he would never fall by the hand of man. Of course, like so many prophecies, this one means something different from what it seems to say, so that he actually falls to a mortal woman and a hobbit.

The Ringwraiths are reminiscent of the Wild Host (or Wild Hunt), the spirits of the dead who ride across the night sky and carry off unwary travellers unable to avoid them. They are a folktale version of the *Einherjar*, the chosen champions of Óðinn who follow him to battle.

A famous passage fom the *Peterborough Chronicle*, a manuscript of the *Anglo-Saxon Chronicle*, for the year 1127 describes the nocturnal procession of a body of Black Riders:

> *Ne þince man na sellice þæt we soð seggen for hit wæs ful cuð ofer eall land þæt swa radlice swa he þær com þæt wæs þes sunendaies þæt man singeð exurge quare OD þa son þær æfter þa segon 7 herdon fela men feole huntes hunten. Ða huntes wæron swearte 7 micele 7 ladlice 7 here hundes ealle swarte 7 bradegede 7 ladlice 7 hi ridone on swarte hors 7 on swarte bucces. Þis wæs segon on þe selue derfald in þa tune on Burch 7 on ealle þa wudes ða wæron fram þa selua tune to Stanforde 7 þa muneces herdon ða horn blawen þæt hi blewen on nihtes. Soðfæste men heom kepten on nihtes sæiden þes þe heom þuhte þæt þær mihte wel ben abuton twenty oðer þritti horn blaweres.*

> Let no man think it strange which we truly tell, since it was well known through all the land that as soon as he [Abbot Henry] came there – that was the Sunday when one sings *Exurge quare O.D.* – then soon thereafter many men saw and heard many hunters hunting. The hunters were black and large and ugly, and their hounds all black and big-eyed and ugly, and they rode on black horses and on black goats. This was seen in the deer-fold itself in the estate at Peterborough and in all the woods which extended from that same estate to Stamford, and the monks heard the horns blowing which they blew at night. Truthful men who kept watch at night said this: that it seemed to them that there might well be around twenty or thirty hornblowers[1].

This cavalacade caused a great deal of concern to the good monks of Peterborough, and the arrival of the Riders was taken as a portent of evil to come.

Rivendell

Rivendell was built by the High Elves in a steep hidden valley near the Misty Mountains. In Rivendell is the House of Elrond, a place of refuge, learning, and wisdom. It is the centre of the power of Elrond, veteran of the struggle with Sauron. Many live in Rivendell who are the bitterest foes of the Dark Lord.

The name may be inspired partly by the Essex place-name Rivenhall, "the rough corner".

---

[1] Text and translation from Pollington, 2000.

Road

The metaphor of the road as a river in Frodo's song *The Road Goes Ever On And On* is one Tolkien used several times to describe the way in which great adventures and home life are not separable: even the longest journey begins with a single step.

Rohirrim

The Rohirrim enter the story as large men clad in mail, with helmets and flowing braided hair, riding tall horses with braided manes. They carry long ash-spears and have shields slung over their backs, and swords at their thighs.

The Rohirrim are the Men of Rohan; both words are based on the Elvish word *roch* 'horse'. The Common Speech words chosen to represent them are unambiguously Old English, noble and equine. Recurrent name-elements include *Eo-* or *Eoh*, two forms of the standard Old English word for 'horse' *eoh*, *eo* and *theod*, Old English *þeod* meaning 'people, tribe, folk'. They call themselves the Eotheod 'horse-folk'. Among their prominent characters are Eomer 'horse-famed', Eowyn 'horse-joy', Eomund 'horse-protector'.

Another Old English word for 'horse' is *mearh* (plural *mearas*) which survives as 'mare' in Modern English.

Their land they named the Riddermark, again from Old English *riddena mearc* 'borderland of the riders'. The tradition of calling the borderlands by the name Mark or March is recalled in the area known as the Welsh Marches, which formed a buffer-zone between England and Wales. However, one of the three most powerful English kingdoms is now called *Mercia*, a Latinised form of the OE *Mierce*, meaning 'men of the Mark', or men of the border. (Tolkien's early homes in the Birmingham region were within historical Mercia, as was his university of Oxford.)

The first king in Rohan was Eorl, a poetic Old English word for a 'leader' or 'hero'. The followers of a leader were, for a period at the beginning of the settlement and creation of England in the post-Roman period, named with the suffix *–ingas* attached the leader's name[1]. For this reason, the leaders of Rohan call themselves also *Eorlingas* 'followers of Eorl'. Due to Danish influence, the word's meaning changed closer to the Scandinavian form *jarl*, a title for a military leader and later for a provincial governor. The modern title 'Earl' has the form of the Old English name but with more of the Danish word's meaning.

The exact nature of the Riders of Rohan has been argued among Tolkien-lovers for decades. Plainly they are intended to represent the early English, and their names and general characteristics confirm this. It is equally clear that Tolkien did not just drop Penda, Offa, Rædwald and the other early English kings into his narrative. The Rohirrim are a blend of the Anglo-Saxons and other elements.

---

[1] This leads to modern place-names such as Barking (*Beorcingas*, followers of the leader Beorc or 'birch-tree'). The settlements were similarly named: *Curringa ham*, home of the followers of Curra, (Corringham) or *Wercinga tun*, settlement of the followers of Werc (Workington).

With their reliance on the horse they resemble some of the East Germanic folk, such as the Goths or Gepids, whose exploits in Central and Southern Europe were known and retold throughout the Germanic world. It is certainly the case that the Rohirrim are not identical to the historical Anglo-Saxons but rather like the Anglo-Saxons in their own myths and legends.

There is yet another strand in the skein, however: there is a hint towards the portrayal of Native Americans in the popular fiction and cinema of the period when Tolkien was growing up. This ranged from the standard 'noble savage' motif to the worthy, implacable foe and ultimately to the native guide – Tonto to the Gondorian Lone Ranger. The Rohirrim are referred to as 'Whiteskins' – a play on the 'Redskins' of the Western genre, perhaps? The details of the attack on the Orcs are also redolent of the early West in cinema – riding round the enemy in a circle and slipping from their horses to silently knife the guards.

Since the story deals with a notionally prehistoric period, it remains possible that Tolkien was drawing in allusions to another group. The English language is a member of the Indo-European family of languages, which is spoken widely throughout Europe and western Asia. The earliest written references to Indo-European-speaking peoples occur in Assyrian texts, where a group called the Mitanni are mentioned. The Mitanni were known even then – two thousand years BC – as expert horsemen and horse-trainers, and the few words of their language recorded in Hittite documents deal with the subject of horse-lore and chariot warfare. It is possible, then, that Tolkien was bringing in such an allusion to demonstrate the kinship of the Mitanni with the 'mythic English', the men of Rohan.

Ruling Ring

See *Rings of Power*

Runestones

There are examples in *The Lord of the Rings* of stones bearing texts and carvings, such as the door of Moria (with its riddling invitation 'say 'friend' and enter') or Balin's Tomb with its commemorative inscription. Stones with formulae indicating who made the monument, who carved it and for whom, are a feature of Scandinavian archaeology from the Roman Iron Age through to late Viking times. The texts are usually in runes. Some of the very earliest ones are no more than a personal name and it is not possible to determine whether this was the maker, recipient or owner of the object.

See below p. 94 for more on runes.

Sam (Samwise) Gamgee

Samwise or 'Sam' Gamgee was a menial gardener in the rural backwater of the Shire but his noble qualities were stirred early on by his love of stories of far-away places and of the Elves. Gandalf suspected that he would make a fine companion for Frodo and instructed them both to leave together for Bree. At the Council of Elrond, he was Elrond's choice of companion for Frodo in the Fellowship. Sam often provides the comic foil to the serious matter of the Ring, yet his inner strength, loyalty and determination shine through as the situation grows more desperate. He takes up the Ring himself, believing Frodo dead, and rescues Frodo from both Shelob and the Orc guards of Cirith Ungol. His unassuming manner, common sense, appreciation of beauty (which he cannot quite put into words) and general firmness contribute as much to the success of Frodo's mission as Frodo's own qualities. On his return to the Shire, Sam was elected Mayor of Michel Delving seven times. He had thirteen children with his sweetheart, Rosie Cotton, and finally passed into the West as the last Ringbearer.

Samwise (*samwis*) is Old English for half-wise, meaning perhaps 'sensible' but not 'educated'. The use of the name enabled Tolkien to give his down-to-earth character a common Modern English forename, 'Sam'.

Saruman

Saruman is one of the three wizards to feature in *The Lord of the Rings*, and at his first appearance he resembles the mediaeval sorcerer or alchemist with his crystal ball (the *palantir*), his private tower and his powerful staff. He was the leader of the wizards' White Council, and was known as Saruman the White. When he repudiated the Council, he adopted a 'coat of many colours' – with strong biblical connotations; and indeed his vanity led to his downfall as surely as in the tale of Joseph.

Saruman's speech, throughout the book, is very 'modern' in comparison with the grandiose language of Elrond or Gandalf. Saruman is persuasive and uses rhetorical devices to sway his listeners. He is plainly modelled on the orators of political movements who can use an array of linguistic tricks to gloss over unpalatable realities.

In many ways, Tolkien seems to regard Saruman as more despicable than Sauron, for he should have known better than to be deceived by the Dark Lord. Saruman loved above all other things the various kinds of mechanical device upon which the modern world is founded.

Saruman is Old English *Searumon* 'cunning man', with resonances of evil since *searu* can mean 'art, skill' but also 'device, instrument of torture'.

Sauron

It was Sauron who had the Rings of Power forged by the Elves. He then made the One Ring – the Ruling Ring – with which to rule the others, making him the Lord of the Rings. He took the form of a fierce warrior - the Dark Lord - but in battle against an alliance of Elves and Men, the Ring was cut from his hand and with that he lost his physical form and much of his power. The background story to *The Lord of the Rings* concerns Sauron's attempt to regain the Ring, and the Fellowship's determination to destroy it.

Sauron is in every sense a shadowy presence, never described fully and taking no direct part in the action of the story. His only physical manifestation is the eye wreathed in flame atop the Dark Tower.

The essence of Sauron's personality is his hunger for control – absolute and total possession – which leads him into the fatal error of failing to perceive the threat posed by the Fellowship. They are not coming against him wielding the Ring in order to supplant him, but instead are intending to destroy the source of his power – and with it that of much of their own well-being which rests on it. With the destruction of the One Ring, the lesser rings of the Elves, Dwarves and men would also fail.

Sauron is associated always with darkness, gloom, shadow in the same way that the most powerful Elves give off light. A dark coloration is usually associated with evil and furtiveness in legend, and in many mythologies black is the colour of death. The northern goddess of the underworld, Hel, for example, was thought to have half her body with pale skin and half with black.

The mythic background to Sauron's Ring is the notion of the magician's 'separable soul' – an object in which he vests a large part of his power, and which is subsequently lost or stolen. Sometimes the thief is a 'culture hero' who recognises the object's power and brings it to earth for the benefit of man. In Norse myth, the weather-god Þórr (Thor, Thunor) has a special belt which confers *jarðarmeginn* 'earth-power' on him, increasing his strength, and a magical hammer which he throws – it never misses, and always returns to his hand. (This hammer is symbolic of the lightning.) Naturally, the hammer is eventually stolen, and the god has to set out on an adventure to recover it.

The 'single baleful eye' motif is an ancient one in northern Europe. The Irish god Balor has a powerful evil eye which he can train on his foes to kill them. Likewise the Norse Óðinn has a single eye, having traded the other for wisdom and the power of prophecy[1].

Shadow

see *Mordor*

Shadowfax

See *Mearas*

Shadowfax (its name means "shadow-mane") is the white horse ridden by Gandalf.

---

[1] This is the Norse tradition recorded by Snorri Sturluson; there is no evidence that the ancient English regarded their counterpart god, Woden, as one-eyed.

Shelob

Gollum had known of Shelob, the great spider, and had passed through her lair, luring others to their deaths in the tunnels to feed her. The Orcs of Mordor had delved routes to avoid her, but always she had found them and fed on the unhappy travellers there. It was Gollum's plan to lure the hobbits to her, and then to retrieve the Ring from the discarded bones and clothing.

Shelob is depicted as a spirit of unrestrained gluttony, a thoroughly selfish and unemotional predator. Sauron had been aware of her lair and found it expedient to leave her there as a watcher; the loss of a few Orcs for her to feed on was no great disadvantage to him. She is depicted as a guardian whom Sauron tolerates since she is so effective at dealing with intruders.

The name was explained by Tolkien as a compound of 'she' (for it is a female) and 'lob', a dialect word for 'spider'.

Shieldwall

At the Battle of Pelennor Fields, a fleet of black-sailed ships appears. As Eomer sees the fleet sailing northwards all hope goes out of his men's hearts, while the enemy are filled with new vigour. Eomer has the horns blown to summon all his men to his banner, intending to make a shieldwall and fight to the last man on foot.

The shieldwall was the standard Anglo-Saxon military formation – a line of infantrymen with shields held before them, their spears presenting a hedge of points to keep back any attacker. Though a strong formation, it could be vulnerable to missile attack.

Ship Burial

There is no time to bury Boromir with due honour, so rather than leaving him in an ignominious grave for passing Orcs to defile, the Fellowship set the nobleman adrift in his boat with treasures and weapons around him.

The rite of ship-burial was known to the Anglo-Saxons and the evidence for it comes from both myth and history: from the Northern myths and from the famous mound 1 at Sutton Hoo, where a king was interred within a 90ft sailing ship. When Óðinn's son Baldur was slain, the gods sent him to the kingdom of Hel laid out in a boat with his father's ring, Draupnir, on his chest. Baldur's boat was set alight and pushed out to sea. However, Boromir is not buried but set adrift on the waters and in this he resembles the mythic ancestor, Scyld Scefing, whose body was placed in a ship's deck surrounded by treasures and set adrift on the waves in the poem *Beowulf*. The poem says " … men do not know how to say truly – neither hall-advisers nor heroes beneath the heavens – who received that cargo." The implication is that Scyld's body and possessions went back to the supernatural powers who had first sent him out onto the sea as a baby.

The single most sumptuous, impressive, expensive and mysterious burial discovered in Britain is that in the famous Mound 1 at Sutton Hoo, Suffolk. It may be the grave of King Rædwald, who died in 625 - this corresponds well with the archaeological dating evidence. The king's ship was hauled to the top of a promontory overlooking the River Deben and lowered into a specially dug hole. The king was laid out with an array of treasures: a helmet, sword, mailcoat, axe and shield; two magnificent drinking horns and several vessels; a lyre and gaming set; a set of hunting and fighting spears; cooking and serving pots and tableware; tapestries and wall-hangings; a curious iron standard and sceptre. A huge mound was raised over the burial, to act as a landmark.

Shire

The Shire is the area of Middle-Earth inhabited by the hobbits. It is divided into four districts – called 'farthings' – and extends westward from the Barrow Downs to the Tower Hills. On its eastern border is the mixed community of Bree, where hobbits live side-by-side with Men.

The vision of the Shire is one of rural England in a pre-Industrial Revolution period. It features farmland, woodland, gently rolling countryside, small hills, ponds and streams (there are no large geographical features such as major rivers or mountains). There are centres of population, all smallish villages such as Hobbiton, Crickhollow, Bywater, etc. There is no heavy industry and the largest machines are wind- and watermills.

The Shire is an idealised version of the southern Midlands English shires. 'Shire' is the Old English word *scir* 'division', based on the word *scieran* 'cut, shear' from which come also *share* 'divided part' and *shears* 'tools for cutting', *shore* 'place where water is divided from land' and *sheer* 'abrupt, sharply divided'. *Farthing* is from OE *feorþing* 'fourth part, quarter'.

Sméagol

See *Gollum*

Song on the Journey

On the journey from Helm's Deep, Merry and King Theoden had exchanged tales but as the journey wears on Merry feels less inclined to talk. He can understand the speech of Rohan only with difficulty. Sometimes a Rider bursts into song and Merry feels a thrill of excitement, though he cannot understand what the singer is saying.

This recalls an incidental detail in the poem *Beowulf*. On the journey from the mere where Beowulf slew Grendel's mother, at times one of the company would sing a song of old legends to entertain the group.

Song of Samwise

In the tower of Cirith Ungol, Sam searches for Frodo. Feeling beyond hope and exhausted after a failed search, he sits on the stairs in darkness. There, all alone in a nest his of enemies, Sam begins to sing a song from the Shire. After a couple of verses he believes he can hear an answering voice.

The motif of the song here recalls the legend of Richard the Lionheart's minstrel, Blondel, who toured Europe trying to find where his lord was imprisoned. His plan was to sing a song they both knew well outside every castle wall until Richard's voice was heard in reply. The ransom for Richard was raised by his mother, Eleanor of Aquitaine, and two leading churchmen. The result was a historical Return of the King.

Sting

Frodo possesses a mystic sword, Sting, given to him by Bilbo. The special quality of the weapon is that it glows in the presence of the enemy (Orcs, trolls or goblins).

Swords which warn of attack are mentioned in Norse, British and Irish myth: the most famous legendary sword, Excalibur, was said to give off a fierce light. This, like much in the Arthurian legends, probably echoes an older, wilder tradition which was recalled in the Ulster Cycle of myth where one hero has a spear which flares up as battle approaches and, if it is not quenched in blood, will turn on its user.

Stone of Erech

In the middle of the night Aragorn and his followers reach the Hill of Erech where a black stone stands – a sphere brought by Isildur out of the west. Aragorn's company gathers at the Stone and he blows a small silver horn; answering blasts come from around.

Prominent landscape features such as marker stones, heathen barrows and even large trees were used as meeting points in Anglo-Saxon times. Such places often formed the central location for a whole district, and would be one of the landmarks from which boundaries were drawn. Numerous Anglo-Saxon charters give the *londgemære* 'land-boundaries' and refer to such easily identifiable features.

Stoors

See *Hobbits*

Strider

Strider is the name Aragorn assumed when in Bree. Aragorn does not reveal his identity to strangers, because he is the heir of Isuldur, last member of the royal line of Arnor.

Heroes often protect their identity with an assumed name. The Norse god Óðinn has dozens of epithets by which he is known in various myths and tales. The name of the Ulster champion Cuchullain is a nick-name 'hound of Cullain' since he undertook the guard duty of the dog he slew. The Greek hero Hercules's local name is *Herakles*, from **hera-klewos* 'fame of (goddess) Hera'.

There is a tradition that the founders of the kingdom of Kent used Hengest and Horsa as by-names – the dynasty was known as the *Oiscingas*, after one Oisc (which may have been the real name of one or other of the brothers).

Swan-Boat

Galadriel's swan-shaped boat which transports her on the Anduin is reminiscent of the swan-maidens of Germanic myth, although these are usually mortal girls who have been enchanted and whose power of flight is confined to an article of clothing.

A similar device, called *fjaðrhama* 'feather-coat', was owned by the goddess Freyja, and was lent to Loki in order to enable him to travel quickly to *Jotunheim* (Giantland) in order to recover Þórr's hammer in the Norse *Þrymskviða*.

Nevertheless, the Old English word *ælfet* means 'swan' and is based on the same root as *ælf* 'Elf': they were both conceived as shining white creatures.

Symbelmyne

The path to the court of Rohan leads over a stream and on past several turf mounds covered with small white flowers, called *symbelmyne,* where the ancestors of Theoden are buried.

The name *symbelmyne* means 'ever-mind' ('constant reminder', or perhaps 'forget-me-not').

Theoden

The first we see of King Theoden is him sitting in his hall, *Meduseld*. The king is thin, aged and bent, with thick white braids issuing from beneath his golden crown. His white beard hangs low on his chest but his eyes are bright and watchful.

Theoden's advisor, Grima (Wormtongue), holds the king under a spell. When Gandalf exposes Grima as a servant of Saruman, the advisor is driven out and Theoden's vigour is restored. When offered his sword, the king grasps the hilt, whirls it through the air and utters the Rohan call to arms.

King Theoden of the Mark comes off the page as the very image of one of the heroes of old. His name is the Old English word for 'lord' particularly describing the lord of a group of freemen (OE *þeod*).

Theoden's assistance with the overthrow of Saruman and the raising of the Siege of Gondor are crucial to the success of the military campaign against Sauron. The old king's last ride to death and glory is for many readers one of the most moving moments in the story.

Theoden's funeral is a very close rendering of a portion of what is known of Germanic burial rites. The building of the king's barrow and the filling of the burial chamber with treasure are evidenced at sites such as Sutton Hoo, Taplow, Broomfield, Asthall and elsewhere in England –as well as in similar graves across Northern Europe. The final memorial drink for Theoden is known from German tradition, where it conveys love of the departed. Oaths accompany strong drink in Germanic culture, and accordingly the funeral drink is the occasion for the engagement (trothplighting) of Faramir and Eowyn.

The final riding round the barrow echoes the funeral of Beowulf, where the fallen leader's companions ride around his barrow singing his praises and mourning his passing.

Thrihyrne

To the south of Rohan lies the mountain with three peaks, called Thrihyrne. The Old English word *ðrihyrne* occurs once in a medical manuscript. It means 'three-horned' or 'three-cornered'.

Thrones of Turves

After their rescue from Mount Doom, Sam and Frodo make their way to an archway of trees where there are mail-clad warriors and an arrangement of seats made from turves, each with a banner behind it. The king is seated on one, with his sword across his knees.

The thrones of turves on which Aragorn, Eomer and Imrahil are seated before their coronation is reminiscent of the traditional royal seat of King Conchobar in the Ulster cycle of myth.

The motif of the king with the naked sword on his knees is drawn from northern customs. It can be seen on the 'king' pieces among the Isle of Lewis chessmen.

Treebeard

See *Ents*

Trolls

The trolls of Middle-Earth are a brutish race: ugly, dull-witted and immensely strong. They are not unlike the giants of folklore, who often have weapons made of stone, or simply uproot a tree as a makeshift club. Some giants were unable to withstand daylight, and would be transformed into stone if it fell upon them. Bilbo Baggins was able to trick the trolls into a lengthy argument in *The Hobbit*, which resulted in their failing to get back underground before the sun came up. The same ruse was used by the god Þórr[1] on the Dwarf Alvis in a Norse legend.

The Old Norse word *troll* describes a class of malevolent beings, more akin to goblins than the stone-trolls of Middle-Earth. One attacked the lands of the

---

[1] Norse Þórr , or Thor, known to the English as Þunor 'thunder'. He gave his name to the fifth day of the week, *Þunresdæg*, Thursday.

legendary King Hrolfr Kraki[1]: it was *mikit ok ógurligt* 'great and terrifying' and no weapon could bite on it. The hero who overcame it – Böðvarr Bjarki, - let his terrified companion drink the beast's blood, after which he was invested with strength and courage and became a great champion of the king's bodyguard.

Two Trees

The Two Trees are the symbol of Gondor, based on the Númenorean tradition of two trees as symbols of life.

The notion has a reflex in Norse myth, where three gods are walking on the seashore and find two pieces of driftwood. Each god endows them with a set of gifts (breath, sight, movement), so that eventually they become living beings, called *Askr* (ash) and *Embla* (elm?), and go on to found the race of men.

Undying Lands

See *Númenor*

Valar.

The *Valar* are subordinates of the creator (demiurges) in the mythology of Middle-Earth, angels or personified aspects of the One. The name *Valar* is a (hardly unintentional) pun on the Norse *valar*, a kind of prophetess or spaewife. To some extent, the Valar are like the Scandinavian Nornir, who are shadowy presences weaving the thread of men's lives into the web of time. They may help or hinder individuals, according to the overall design.

Warfare

A large part of the appeal of *The Lord of the Rings* is based on the fascinating way in which Tolkien manages to evoke the flavour of the mediaeval European world without ever merely replicating the specifics of it. This can be seen in, for example, the military equipment. We are not given any clear and detailed descriptions of the many weapons and other kinds of equipment available to the different races in the tale, yet the feeling throughout is that the war-gear is characteristic of the early mediaeval period. While one would not wish to confine it very closely, there are suggestive details that indicate the range 800-1200 AD – a formative period in the history of Western Europe, taking in the Viking Age, the Holy Roman Empire and the earlier Crusades.

For most groups, the principal form of body armour is the mailcoat and helm. This is true of England and northern Europe from the late Iron Age through to the end of the Norman period. (The most spectacular English example of these two items in conjunction is the Sutton Hoo ship burial, with its magnificent helm and rivetted mailcoat, both badly corroded after 1500 years in the soil.) Some individuals have better armour - such as the mithril mailcoat Frodo

[1] The text is given in Garmonsway, 1928.

wears. Like a Kevlar vest, mithril confers a good deal of protection on the hobbit, although like all mail it is most useful against slashing and hacking blows but cannot prevent a concussion injury.

The Knights of Dol Amroth are described as wearing plate armour, which makes its earliest appearance in northern Europe in the 1200s, although there are precursors: the Swedish Vendel graves of the 6th century feature protection for the shins and forearms in the form of narrow iron strips, which may also be depicted on English artefacts such as the 8th century Franks Casket. The Haradrim are described as wearing armour of overlapping plates, which may recall the *lorica segmentata* (overlapping iron hoops) of the Roman infantry. Orc armour is considered heavy and unwieldy, and the Orc captain in Moria has a large shield made of hide as well as a full coat of mail.

The guards of Minas Tirith have a livery of black and silver, which is used on the surcoats they wear over their mailcoats. Surcoats are characteristic of the High Middle Ages, and are most noticeably used by Crusaders to protect their metal armour from the sun. With the adoption of larger helmets, covering the face entirely, the surcoat was used to display identification marks, which developed in time into a system of heraldry.

Shields are described as broad or round, and decorated with 'heraldic' devices. Round shields are characteristic of Northern Europe – the Anglo-Saxons, Vikings, Lombards and Carolingian Franks all used circular boards, with a central boss protecting the hand. The Rohirrim use the decorative device of a green field with a running horse. The Orcs' shields and other equipment are embellished with their two devices: the White Hand of Saruman, or the Lidless Red Eye of Sauron.

Weaponry consists of swords, knives, spears and bows. Some groups, such as the Dwarves and the Easterlings, use broad-bladed axes. All these weapons are characteristic of European warfare from the early Iron Age through to the Norman periods – they are depicted in the Bayeux Tapestry, for example. Bows do not appear to have been a favoured weapon of English forces at this time, but there are occasional references to their use in war (e.g. the poem *The Battle of Maldon* says *bogan wæron bysige* 'bows were busy').

Orcs are described as wielding curved scimitars – a weapon typical of the Islamic foes of the Crusaders. However, curved swords were used in Europe from early times: the *falcata* of the early Iron Age, for example, or the mediaeval *falchion*. These were often single-edged, like the fearsome *seax* of the Saxons.

There is a suggestion of gunpowder having been developed by the 'modernising' troops of Saruman and Sauron. It is used at Helm's Deep by Saruman's Orcs to blast a breach in the Deeping Wall. Again, at the Siege of Gondor, Sauron's Orcs use something similar to demolish the Rammas protective wall. The latter also have siege towers, siege catapults and a huge battering ram. All these latter weapons were familiar to the Romans, and while the evidence for their continued use throughout the early Middle Ages is not conclusive, they were certainly available to armies of the Crusades.

Wargs

When the Fellowship is attacked by savage wolves or wargs, the warg-leader dies on one of Legolas's arrows and the attacks cease. In the morning, no bodies of the creatures can be found and the spent arrows are lying undamaged on the ground. This convinces Gandalf that the animals are not flesh and blood but rather some uncanny sending of Sauron's.

The *wargs* are overgrown wolves, used as mounts by the Orcs of Saruman. The word *warg* (Old English *wearg*, Mercian *warg*) is a related form of the word *wulf* 'wolf'. It denotes, in surviving Old English records, an outlaw or bandit, a proverbial 'lone wolf'.

Waybread

When the Fellowship are about to leave Lothlorien, some Elves come to them with supplies for the journey: food and clothing. Some of the food is in the form of thin biscuits, called *lembas* or 'waybread', which is baked hard to be taken on long journeys where the sources of food are uncertain. It is light and delicious, and very nutritious; one of them can sustain a full-grown man for a day.

The *lembas* or 'waybread' the Fellowship are given is a typical Tolkien pun: the plant-name 'waybread' is from OE *wegbræd* and has nothing to do with bread. The name describes its broad (*brad*, *bræd*) leaves and its common habitat by the path (*weg*, *wæg*).

The West

See *Journey into the West* and *Númenor*

"Westu Theoden hal!"

Eomer's greeting to his lord, Theoden, is a variant of Beowulf's greeting to Hroþgar: *Wæs þu Hroþgar hal* when he is finally allowed to address the king directly. Its meaning is rendered as "Theoden, be thou hale" but in fact this traditional form of words is a wish for wholeness, health and good luck, all rendered by the Old English word *hal*.

White Council

The White Council is the congress of Istari or wizards. Its leader is Saruman, whose knowledge of Sauron and the Ring is unrivalled. Unfortunately, his study of the Dark Lord convinces Saruman that defeat is inevitable unless it is possible to seize the Ruling Ring and use it against the enemy. This leads him to develop plans to challenge Sauron, to breed a race of mutant Orcs and to try to conquer areas of Middle-Earth for himself.

In time, Saruman's white garment is refracted into a 'coat of many colours' and he begins to move against Elrond. The White Council is then dissolved, as Saruman no longer feels himself accountable to his peers.

Withywindle

See *Old Man Willow* and *Tom Bombadil*

The strangest and most dangerous part of the Old Forest is the Withywindle valley. As Frodo, Sam, Merry and Pippin travel through the wood, they find that they are being edged eastwards towards the river valley, and however much they try to correct their course, the way rightwards and downwards is always easier. Soon they are lost and it is apparent that they are being gently ushered into the valley of the Withywindle, the heart of the Forest itself.

The name 'Withywindle' appears to be made from two elements: 'withy' from OE *wiðig* 'willow tree' and 'windle' from OE *windan* 'to wind, turn, twist'. This is logical enough given the willow-crowded nature of the river and its lazy, winding course. However, the word is very close in sound and form to OE *wiðowinde* 'bindweed, convulvulus' the plant which chokes other vegetation and structures by wrapping and coiling itself around them.

Wizards

In *The Lord of the Rings* there were five *Istari* or wizards in all, though only three are named: Saruman, Radagast and Gandalf. See the entries for each of the wizards.

Wood or Water?

In Minas Tirith, Legolas is sad, because he has been near the sea and that knowledge awakes a longing in all Elves to go seafaring, so that he will never be happy again in the woods. On reaching the mouth of the river Anduin, Legolas hears seabirds and recalls the warning of Galadriel to beware the cry of the gulls.

When Legolas speaks of the yearning he has for the sea, he recalls the sentiment of the Old English poem *The Seafarer*, which tells of the great fear a mariner feels out in his little ship on the ocean, but the overwhelming longing he feels when he has stayed a while on land. The motif of the dilemma of the Elves – love of the woodland or love of the sea – echoes the Norse tale of the marriage of the god Njorðr and the goddess Skaði. He is a coastal dweller and cannot sleep in the wolf-haunted forests, while she is a mountain-dweller and hates the mewing of the gulls in the fjords. The antipathy may reflect the uneasy alliance between those who live by fishing and those who live by hunting.

There is, furthermore, a range of Old English words for different kinds of Elf, including Wood-Elves and Water-Elves. This may have been at the back of Tolkien's mind in this passage – the Old English vocabulary suggests a range of beings while Tolkien, characteristically, weaves these into a tradition of sea-yearning drawn from the imagery of *The Seafarer*.

Woses

See *Dunharrow* and *Púkel-Men*

The Woses, the Wild Men of the Druadan Forest, are simple folk who live by hunting in the woods. Similar to the Dunlendings, the Woses are the original inhabitants of the area later known as the Riddermark. The Riders had hunted them in the past, so that they had become very wary of contact with other races of men. They are described as primitive, small and gnarled – a caricature perhaps of some aboriginal people who have been marginalized to the point where they are no longer believed to exist. While they have something of the Noble Savage about them, their contribution to the story is to show that even the least developed of human races is still sentient, can choose between right and wrong, and has its part to play in the great struggle of the Free Peoples.

The name *Wose* is based the Old English word *wuduwosa* 'wood-being' which denoted a kind of legendary spirit of the woods, perhaps akin to the Green Man. The name *wuduwosa* may survive in the surname Woodhouse. In *The Lord of the Rings* they are named Púkel-men, derived from Old English *pucca*, *puccel* 'goblin, brownie' (perhaps connected with the verb *pucian* 'creep'?). Related terms occur in Old Irish *púca* 'spirit' which may have given rise to the Old English word. Shakespeare's woodland spirit Puck in *A Midsummer Night's Dream* and Kipling's *Puck of Pook's Hill* are also derivatives of the same idea.

Woses' Reckoning

See *Dunharrow*

In Druadan Forest, Ghan-buri-Ghan, king of the Woses, tells Theoden that there are more men gathered on the road than there are Riders to fight them. The number of Riders has been ascertained, much to Eomer's amazement, as well as the size of the enemy forces on the road and at the city.

The Wose numbers the Riders as a "score of scores counted ten times and five" i.e. (20 x 20) x 15 = 6,000. The use of the ancient numeric 'score' (twenty, the sum of one person's fingers and toes) indicates the archaic nature of the Woses' tradition of thought – which is nevertheless accurate.

4. The Languages of the People of Middle-Earth

The expert use of multi-layered languages in the narrative is one of the hallmarks of Tolkien's writing. Not only do all the various peoples of Middle-earth have their own languages, but there are ancient and modern variants, alongside dialects and garbled forms.[1]

In common with other fine writers, Tolkien subtly adjusted the pace and wording of his narrative to suit the needs of the story. He also managed to suggest something of the character of the various peoples through the sounds they use – the soft, mellifluous harmonies of the Elves; the harsh gutturals of the Dwarves; the archaic English of the Rohirrim; the long-winded, sonorous booming of the ents; the feral croaking and growling of the Orcs.

As Modern English is necessarily used to represent Westron, the Common Speech which is spoken and understood as a *lingua franca* by all Free Peoples, and as the narrative is universally told from the hobbits' point of view, it follows that the nature of the English used by any group reflects their relationship to the hobbits. Perhaps least striking but most effective is the way that Tolkien uses a dignified form of English, based mainly on Old English, to convey qualities he admired: honesty, closeness to nature, dignity and reserve. The hobbit's speech is a slightly rustic form of this. Due to the ancient speech of Wilderland having given rise to Westron and to the language of the men of Rohan, this group uses archaic and formal Old English throughout the book. The men of Gondor are more 'elevated' in their language, meaning that they use the French- and Latin-based vocabulary of the English-speaking educated classes, reflecting the Gondorians' familiarity with Elvish (represented by Latin, perhaps).

Not content with an original invented, Elvish language Tolkien devised at least two divergent forms to be used by different branches of the Elves: Quenya-speaking Quendi and Sindarin-speaking Sindar. Elvish words escaped into the language of the Gondorians, and even that of the Orcs.

Sindarin 'grey-elvish' was the language of the western Elves. The Gondorians and the Dúnedain used this tongue informally, and their names reflect this:

---

[1] Using the evidence of the Proto-Eldarin and later Elvish languages, it has been possible for one scholar to attempt to find Elvish loanwords in the oldest strata of the ancient Indo-European language group (the ancestor of most modern European languages and of many in the Indian sub-continent). This would place contact between Elvish-speakers and ancient Europeans around 5,000 BC. This is just one method used to determine the period of human history Tolkien had in mind when writing the books.

Aragorn, Denethor and so on. Quenya was an older and more elevated form of language. *Elessar*, the adopted royal title of Aragorn, is a Quenya name.

Quenya

The Quenya language was brought to Middle-Earth by the Elves from their home in the West. It is based systematically on an original Elvish tongue, known to Tolkien students as Proto-Eldarin. Tolkien based Quenya's structure on Finnish, a language with which he fell in love on learning it. Quenya is characterised by a very full system of grammar (perhaps nine cases for the noun, three tenses for the verb) of a type usually found in very old or very conservative languages. Its use in *The Lord of the Rings* is parallel to Latin in Western Europe: an ancient language used in formal and religious contexts.

An example of Quenya from *The Fellowship of the Ring* is the greeting: *Elen síla lúmenn' omentielvo* "a star shines at the hour of our meeting".

Sindarin

Sindarin is the language of the Grey Elves, and was adopted by the first Men. It fragmented into a number of dialects with regional flavours, so that the speech of different communities diversified away from the original standard. The model for Sindarin was ancient and modern Welsh, a language Tolkien studied and which he thought contained a large proportion of beautiful words. The grammar appears to be rather simpler than that of Quenya, but Tolkien introduced a tell-tale Welsh feature: known as *lenition*, it is the process by which Welsh words change their initial sounds. (For example, *ci* means 'dog' but a specific kind of small dog is a *cor* – *gi* 'dwarf dog, corgi' – the *c* becomes a *g* in some circumstances. 'My dog' is *fy nghi*, and there are other distortions of the initial sounds. This feature is common to all known Insular Celtic languages.)

Sindarin is a more modern language than Quenya, and is the everyday medium of conversation among the various groups of Elves.

An example of Sindarin is Gandalf's attempted opening spell on the doors of Moria: *Annon edhellen, edro hi ammen! Fennas nogothrim, lasto beth lammen!* "Elvish gate open now for us; doorway of the Dwarf-folk listen to the word of my tongue!"

Khuzdul (Dwarvish)

Khuzdul is the secret language of the Dwarves, which they do not share with outsiders. It is only scantily recorded in the books, but appears to be structured like modern Arabic or Hebrew, with roots formed from three consonants, into which vowels are inserted to provide shades of meaning. One productive root is *k^hzd* 'Dwarf' which gives rise to *Khazâd* 'Dwarves', *Khazad-* 'Dwarvish', *Khuzdul* 'Dwarvish language'. It is a guttural language, harsh and abrupt.

An example of Dwarvish is Gimli's exclamation: *Baruk Khazâd!* "Axes of the Dwarves!"

Black Speech

This is the language of Mordor, promoted by Sauron in the Second Age and revived in the Third Age – which ends with the War of the Ring – for use as a *lingua franca* among the various races serving the Dark Lord. The only two examples of the language are the inscription on the Ruling Ring, and the curse uttered by one of Sauron's Orcs against the Uruk-hai. The commonest Black Speech word in the book is probably *Nazgûl* "Ringwraith" based on *nazg* 'ring', *gûl* 'magic'. The inscription on the Ruling Ring reads: *Ash nazg durbatulûk, ash nazg gimbatul, ash nazg thrakatulûk agh burzum-ishi krimpatul.* "One Ring to rule them all, One Ring to find them, One Ring to bring them all and in the Darkness bind them."

Westron

Westron is the *lingua franca* of Middle-Earth and is understood by all races, even those such as the Ents that have little to do with the outside world. Its true name is *Adunaic*, after its speakers, the *adûn* '(men of the) West' – hence "Westron". It is represented by Modern English throughout the books, but a few examples are given of the original tongue: *pharaz* for 'gold', for example, or *banakil* for 'hobbit'.

Entish

The language of the Ents is described as "slow, sonorous, agglomerated, repetitive, indeed long-winded". With characteristic aversion to hastiness, the language appears to be highly specific and repetitive. The name for one 'knoll' is seven words and fifteen syllables long: *a-lalla-lalla-rumba-kamanda-lindor-burúmë* is the only extended example of Entish given in the book, although there are moments when Fangorn lapses into his mother tongue when describing the Orcs. At the Entmoot, Tolkien says "the Ents began to murmur slowly: first one joined and then another, until they were all chanting together in a long rising and falling rhythm, now louder on one side of the ring, now dying away there and rising to a great boom on the other side". The discussion was presumably a protracted, harmonic mingling of many voices, resulting at last in a single chanted conclusion.

Writing

There are two principal forms of writing employed in *The Lord of the Rings*, the Elves' *Tengwar* and the Dwarves' *Cirth*. Perhaps it should come as no surprise to learn that both are based on genuine Anglo-Saxon scripts, the bookhand and the runestaves or *fuþorc* respectively.

The Tengwar.

The Elvish writing known as the Tengwar is loosely based on the Anglo-Saxon bookhand script. Tolkien was familiar with the details of Anglo-Saxon orthography and understood well the problems of interpretation a single badly-formed character can produce. For the Tengwar, he took the formal shape of the bookhand – long, graceful ascenders and descenders with loops and hooks to left or right - and transformed them into a logical system of speech transcription. This must rank as a unique achievement in English literature!

Tolkien used more than one form of the script; in fact, he seems to have revised his ideas about the best usage periodically. He opted, for example, for vowels represented by marks over the preceding consonants (as in modern Arabic script) but realised that the system would not work perfectly when a vowel begins a word (i.e. there is no *preceding* consonant). He got round this difficulty by devising an 'empty' placeholder for the vowels, though he also developed full vowel letters. He used diacritics to show a preceding nasal, a following sibilant, or a doubled consonant.

As a practical writing system, the Tengwar is of limited use because it has insufficient redundancy – there is not enough distinction between individual letters for a poorly crafted text to be readable. Yet the Tengwar was invented for and by Elves, whose immortality lent them infinite patience and care in producing documents and inscriptions, and for whom elegance was everything.

The principal Tengwar letters are given opposite. Below are the standard Anglo-Saxon bookhand forms.

Standard Anglo-Saxon (English) Bookhand

a	a	f	ꝼ	m	m	s	ꞅ	y	ẏ
b	b	g	ᵹ	n	n	t	ꞇ	th	þ
c	c	h	h	o	o	u	u	th	ð
d	ꝺ	i	ı	p	p	w	ƿ	æ	æ
e	e	l	l	r	ꞃ	x	x	&	⁊

Note: both þ and ð could stand for the sounds we write 'th', as in 'thin' and in 'this'.

Standard Elvish Tengwar Bookhand

t	p	p	ꝑ	k	q	k^w	q
d	pɔ	b	ꝑɔ	g	ɯq	g^w	ɯq
þ	h	f	b	k^h	d	h^w	d
ð	hɔ	v	bɔ	g^h	ɯd	g^{hw}	ɯd
m	mɔ	n	ɯɔ		ɯı		ɯı
r	ɒ	w	ɒ	y	ɑ		ɑ
r^2	ɣ	r^h	ɣ	l	ꞇ	l^h	ꞅ
s	ϭ	s	9	z	ϭ	z	ʒ
h	λ	w^h	d	y	ʌ	w	o

Note: Here þ stands for the sounds we write 'th', as in 'thin' and ð as in 'this'.

In addition to these forms there is the 'empty' vowel-carrier ȷ and some characters which extend above and below the line, such as þɔ or ꝑ . A variant spelling system was derived from the Quenya standard for Sindarin. A further development was for the Black Speech – for example, the inscription on the Ruling Ring itself.

The principles underlying the construction, relative values and development of these characters are given in Appendix E to *The Lord of the Rings*. It is evident that the starting point was the Anglo-Saxon bookhand, tidied up and made more logical through Tolkien's philological training. Obvious formal parallels include:

English Bookhand	*Elvish Tengwar*	*English Bookhand*	*Elvish Tengwar*
ƿ	p	m	mɔ
b	b	n	ɒ
ʒ	ꞅ	o	o
ꞇ	ꞇ	u	ɑ
h	h	ꞃ	ꝑ
ẏ	ɣ	ꝺ	d
ꞁ	ȷ		

The Cirth.

Runestaves are of unknown antiquity. The oldest inscriptions date to around the time of the birth of Christ, but they already showed some developments in the spelling tradition, suggesting that they were no longer a novelty even then. The earliest runestaves are known as the *fuþark* after the first six characters; the later English version is known as the *fuþorc*. Old Norse tradition assigns them a divine origin – they were seized by the god Óðinn after nine nights of deprivation on the World Tree. Runestaves are characterised by long upright strokes with short angular branches attached to, usually, the right side.

The Dwarvish Cirth formally resembles the Anglo-Saxon *fuþorc* in many of its characters, although the phonetics are very different.

In *The Hobbit*, Tolkien took over genuine Anglo-Saxon runestaves directly, with minimal modification, for the Dwarves' map and for the endpapers of the book. They offer an air of northern antiquity and, since the text of Thrain's message is given in the story, the reader can actually figure out the correspondences and transliterate the runic script.

The Cirth is set out opposite, alongside the standard Anglo-Saxon *fuþorc*, and the special characters used in *The Hobbit*.

Standard Anglo-Saxon (English) Fuþorc or Rune-Row

f	ᚠ	h	ᚻ	t	ᛏ	a	ᚪ
u	ᚢ	n	ᚾ	b	ᛒ	æ	ᚫ
þ	ᚦ	i	ᛁ	e	ᛖ	y	ᚣ
o	ᚩ	(j)	ᛄ	m	ᛗ	ea	ᛠ
r	ᚱ	æ	ᛇ	l	ᛚ	k’	ᛤ
c	ᚳ	(z)	ᛉ	ng	ᛝ	g’	ᚸ
g	ᚷ	p	ᛈ	d	ᛞ	st	ᛥ
w	ᚹ	s	ᛋ	œ	ᛟ		

Note: k’, g’ denote palatalised variants of the standard runes. These only appear epigraphically in Northumbria.

Tolkien's Dwarf-Runes are identical to the Anglo-Saxon runes above except in the following respects:

Exceptional Dwarf Runes

ᛟ	ee	used for the vowel in the word 'feet'; this is not so much an innovation, since in Old English the word *fet* replaced *fœt* as the plural of *fot* 'foot'. (The rune ᛟ had the sound 'o' originally.)
ᚫ	a	used with the value 'a' whereas in Old English it has the value 'æ'; the rune ᚪ is 'a' in Old English
ᛞ	d	instead of the usual Old English ᛞ
Z	eo	used to spell the name 'George'; a rune of this shape appears in some Old English manuscripts

Angerthas Cirth Rune-Row

	p		z^h		l		e
	b		n^j/z		l^h		é
	f		k		n^g/nd		a
	v		g		s/h		á
	h^w		k^h		s/'		o
	m		g^h		z/n^g		ó
	m^h		n^g/n		ng		ö
	t		k^w		nd/n^j		n
	d		g^w		i/y		h/s
	þ		k^{hw}		y		-
	ð		g^{hw}		h^y		-
	n/r		n^{gw}		u		ps
	c^h		n^w		ú		ts
	j		r/j		w		h
	s^h		r^h/z^h		ü		&

The Cirth was developed along parallel lines to the Tengwar, so that ᚹ corresponded to p and so on.

The following signs occur in both English and Dwarvish systems:

ᚹ ᚱ ᛒ ᛚ ᚫ ᛏ ᚳ ᛦ ᚴ ᚠ ᛘ ᛈ ᚼ ᚷ ᛝ ᛁ ᛋ ᛟ ᛟ ᚻ ᚢ ᚦ ᛚ

The following are runic variants from Old English or other languages (e.g. Old Norse) also found in the Cirth:

ᛉ ᛯ ᚲ ᛞ ᛜ ᚺ ᚢ ᚼ ᚿ

Interestingly, the name *Balin* on the Moria tomb ᚱ ᚢ ᚾ ᛁ ᛘ appears to spell out the word 'runic' in a combination of genuine Germanic letters.

Calendars

With his deep love of language Tolkien combined a liking for astronomy and time-reckoning. He used this to good effect in the creation of a wonderfully consistent Shire Calendar which appears in *The Return of the King* as Appendix D.

Briefly, each of the twelve Shire months has 30 days. To this total of (12x30=) 360 month-days are added five additional days which stand outside the months: two at midwinter and three at midsummer.

This system is based closely on the true Anglo-Saxon reckoning, which made use of 'intercalary days' outside the months. These were known as *liþa* 'midsummer' and *geola* 'Yule, midwinter'. Tolkien brought these up to date as *Lithe* and *Yule* in Modern English.

The month-names are also based on the corresponding Old English names:

	Old English	**Meaning**	**Shire**
1	*se æfterra geola*	the later Yule	Afteryule
2	*solmonað*	sun (?)-month	Solmath
3	*hreðmonað*	fierce(?)-month	Rethe
4	*eastron*	Easter	Astron
5	*ðrymilce*	three-milking	Thrimidge
6	*se ærra liða*	the earlier Lithe	Forelithe
7	*se æfterra liða*	the later Lithe	Afterlithe
8	*weodmonað*	weed-month	Wedmath
9	*haligmonað*	holy-month	Halimath
10	*winterfulleð*	winter full-moon	Winterfilth
11	*blotmonað*	blood-month	Blotmath
12	*se ærra geola*	the earlier Yule	Foreyule

The designations of the Old English months are practical. For examples, May is 'three milking' based on dairy practice, when cows can be milked three times a day. November is 'blood-month' as it is the time when stock, which will not be kept alive over winter, is slaughtered.

5. Where are the English in the 'Mythology for England'?

What is the relationship between the various characters and groups in *The Lord of the Rings* and the English, for whom the work was written? It is not reasonable to assume that Tolkien went to all the trouble of inventing and devising a 'mythology for England' without including the English in it. Yet he could no more insert historical persons into the mythic narrative, then Ian Fleming could drop Beowulf into a James Bond novel. While both are fiction, the literary modes are totally different, and so are the expectations of their readers. So, however he would accomplish it, the English in the tale would have to be adapted to the particular circumstances of his narrative.

As a professional historian of the English language, Tolkien knew very well the processes of formation and change which have resulted in the modern language - and the social developments which accompanied them. He carefully matched ancient features (old words, old word-orders) to older characters: Elrond and Gandalf especially are marked by this device when they discuss the Ring at the Council in Rivendell. Having adopted the posture of 'translator' of an ancient manuscript he was obliged to pursue the fiction by maintaining a relationship between the languages and styles of the various groups in Middle-Earth through their Modern English forms. (This does not work entirely well, since he was obliged to give the two forms of Elvish, Dwarvish and the Black Speech of Mordor in the original. Also, if the equation Westron = Modern English is adopted, then among the speakers of Westron must be the speakers of Modern English. Yet the almost unknown hobbits could not have disseminated their own language to groups of Men and made it the *lingua franca* of the entire continent, in the way that the English spread their language around the world.)

Setting aside the inconsistencies arising from this problem, there are three groups in the book whose claim to represent the English seems fairly clear. First, of course, are the hobbits, who are in every scene the readers' surrogates. They evince modern attitudes, dress in modern clothes, use modern manners (modern for the time at which the book was written) and act as interpreters of the various strands of story.

Hobbits are sturdy, earth-fast and quiet; not grand or powerful but tenacious and unyielding. Their quiet good humour, love of comfort and tranquility and ability to withstand as much misfortune as the world can throw at them without despairing are all attributes of the rural English.

The second group are the Rohirrim who are clearly intended to be the "Anglo-Saxons" - which is to say the ancestors of the English. Tolkien denied that this was so, since he wanted to maintain the fiction of an ancient text in which the historical English could have no place. Yet, despite his protestations, it is clear to most readers that there is a fundamental similarity between the men of Rohan and the early English. That 'similarity' approaches but does not reach 'identity' is down to Tolkien's skill as a narrator and to the small twist which he gave to the story in making the Rohirrim dependant upon their horses. In their original homeland (northern Germany and the Jutland peninsula) the *Anglii*, as they then called themselves, were among many groups whose contact with the Roman Empire encouraged them to expand. Some of these groups moved south, took to the plains of eastern Europe and became great horsemen able to match the nomads of the Steppe who were their close companions from the 3rd century AD onwards. (The traditions of Attilla the Hun are recorded in many Germanic languages.) Other groups moved west, using boats and ships to travel along the North Sea coasts; some made the short crossing to Britain. Among these were the leaders of the Anglii. (There were other groups of Anglii who did move south, perhaps earlier, but whose history is lost apart from scraps of tradition and an occasional mention in later histories.) For this reason, the Angles who came to Britain – to create Angle-land, *Englaland*, England – were not horse-based but ship-based for their transport needs.

The Rohirrim are more akin to the ideas the Angles had of themselves in their legends, and the virtues of the Riders are the same virtues which the Angles admired and respected: courage, loyalty, generosity, self-reliance. An Old English adage says *eorl sceal on eos boge* "a hero belongs on a horse's back", stressing the association they felt between the adventures of the hero and his reliable mount. Another states *guð sceal in eorle* "warfare is proper for a hero".

There is a possible third category of persons who might be characterised as typically English: the Wizards. In *The Lord of the Rings* they are the priest-kings of their society, involved and concerned with the affairs of the free folk but not entirely engaged and dependant. (If everything should go wrong in Middle-Earth, the wizards may withdraw and recommence their struggle at a later date.) Gandalf's slightly grumpy good-nature is counterpoised by Saruman's unctuous double-dealing. Saruman is clearly a career politician, a leader who claims to serve the community while really serving no-one's interests but his own. (While this characteristic is not uniquely English, the subsequent history of Saruman in spoiling the Shire can hardly be anything other than a comment on the plans of a great mind to undo a perfectly adequate system and replace it with corruption and waste, in the name of progress. The reader is free to pick a modern leader of whatever political hue who has behaved in this manner.)

If these three groups are considered as a whole – hobbits, riders and wizards – then they conform to an ancient model of society. King Alfred the Great wrote that his kingdom needed *gebedmen 7 fyrdmen 7 weorcmen* "praying men and fighting men and working men", the three degrees of mediaeval society. The wizards stand in the place of priests and kings, being concerned with leadership, planning and the spiritual and magical dimension. The Men of the

Riddermark correspond to the warriors, concerned with defence and controlled use of force. The hobbits, as rural agriculturalists, denote the underpinning workforce of their society.

6. A Mythology for All Middle-Earth?

The Lord of the Rings is a book intended to provide an escape from the modern world, an antidote to the spiritual poison of consumerism and materialism and the relentless, dreary uniformity of socialism in the early 20th century. Tolkien was an opponent of the 'planned' society espoused by social engineers, which caused so much misery when the planning was hopelessly out-of-touch with human needs. The anti-industrial message in so much of Tolkien's writings pre-figured the anti-capitalist 'green' movement of more recent times.

There is a certain irony in its having been voted the greatest work of literature of the 20th century, when so little of the 20th century appears in it. Tolkien seems to have put his finger on something deeply significant about the psychological needs of modern western society, and to have found a way to explore these needs creatively.

Evidently many people are unmoved by what he has to say, and find the whole enterprise silly or trivial. The fact that the author was a middle-aged, middle-class male academic with a deep love for his country only adds fuel to the flames of their dislike. (A sensible academic at an English university ought to have no business loving England and the English, the language, the countryside, the way of life.)

The Monsters and the Critics

The appeal of the books is hard to define. One author of mass-market fantasy fiction remarked that at the age of fifteen everyone should love *The Lord of the Rings*, and by the age of twenty-five no-one should still like it. That is an interesting point, since it implies that the books can only speak to a group in the mid-teens to mid-twenties age range. There are, of course, many fantasy works of which that statement is true, but *The Lord of the Rings* is not one of them.

The story may have appeal to the teenage power fantasies of male adolescents – particularly Aragorn, the despised loner who hides a secret and amazing power which he finally reveals to overthrow an established order. For females, there are perhaps few real models in the books, unless one counts the action heroine Eowyn or the beautiful and demur ruler Galadriel. But the standard sword-and-sorcery characters and set-piece situations of modern fiction are for the most part pale imitations of Tolkien, by writers with limited imagination and powers of expression.

A criticism levelled at many fantasy works is that the 'characters' are not characters at all, they are mere ciphers, stereotyped and unconvincing. This is often true these days: since *The Lord of the Rings* broke the mould for fantasy writing, almost every author since includes certain stock elements: "stubborn Dwarves", "graceful Elves", and not a few have "determined halflings" too. Tolkien's characters do develop, though, and not always in directions that are predictable when they first enter the story. Aragorn starts out as indecisive and wayward, and grows more confident and responsible as the tale progresses. Boromir, in contrast, enters the tale as a confident leader, and gradually loses his strength of will as the Ring acts on his ego. Denethor, though not in the story for long, crumbles from a shrewd and cunning potentate to a despairing old man. Gimli begins as suspicious and irascible, but the encounter with Galadriel softens him, and sparks a love for the Lady that reverses his previous convictions about the Elves. Saruman is early on a powerful force, able to overcome Gandalf with ease, but by the end is a bitter, resentful and malicious wayfarer. The profound transformations in Gandalf (from member of an order of wizards to leader of the West), Theoden (from wizened patriarch to vigorous warrior) and Frodo (from carefree rural landowner to Ringbearer and saviour of the West) are central to the story.

One aspect of the narrative which Tolkien handles particularly well is nostalgia, longing, the sense of great loss and sadness as cherished and beautiful things pass beyond reach. Such themes inform a lot of great literature, and they stand behind the author of *Beowulf*'s attempt to marry up the lost world of Germanic legend with the reality of Christian England. The nostalgia the hobbits feel for their quiet, uneventful lives in the Shire probably reflects something from Tolkien's personal WWI experience: the longing of troops, drawn from rural areas of England, for their homes and families, away from the mud, squalor, disease and pain of life in the trenches.

There is, however, a deeper sense of loss displayed in the profound sadness of the Elves whose part in the War of the Ring must lead to the downfall of all they love in Middle-Earth. While the Elves have great and lasting affection for the trees and natural landscape of their domain, they also recognise their wider duty to their fellow creatures, and they are willing, in the end, to give up all they have in order that others may continue to enjoy it. The bitter surrender is all the more poignant since they know they must dwindle from a position of mastery to become little more than the stuff of childish tales.

Radio

Both *The Lord of the Rings* and *The Hobbit* have been adapted for radio by the BBC and subsequently released on tape. The stories work well, adapted to the sound-only format. However, despite performances by some fine character actors, the adaptation of the *Rings* was rather ponderous and overdone. The lack-lustre, mock-mediaeval introductory music sets the tone for the adaptation. Despite, or perhaps because of this, neither radio production has met with the strong reaction accorded to the films. It is clearly less disturbing for Bilbo or Treebeard to sound different from our expectations than it is for these characters to both look and sound different.

Films

Directing and producing a film of *The Lord of the Rings* is a little like managing a national football squad: every bar in the country is full of experts on the subject, yet they still manage to give the job to the one man who is incapable of doing it properly!

For those who love the books – in many cases passionately – no film version is ever going to be satisfactory. No presentation of much-loved characters on the screen – old friends who have kept us company for many years – can ever match the personal recollection we have of them. Anybody adapting *The Lord of the Rings* for another medium is automatically likely to disappoint and alienate a large proportion of his potential audience before he has begun work. The very suggestion of altering *The Lord of the Rings* is as unthinkable as altering the Koran or Holy Writ is to religious fundamentalists. It becomes absolutely a matter of principle not to change the received text.

The first cinematic release purporting to bring *The Lord of the Rings* to the big screen was Ralph Bakshi's animated adventure. The film began promisingly and kept reasonably close to the books. Novel animation techniques were deployed, involving the use of live-action characters (subsequently 'posterised' to render them more menacing and to blend them in with their celluloid surroundings) along with more traditional methods. The result was nevertheless disappointing: the sombre live-action figures were difficult to discern, while all the animated characters were over-exposed, leading to a very jarring visual contrast. Even more unforgivable was the way the film took so long to reach the battle of Helm's Deep, then suddenly ended! Tolkien fans reacted with a vigorous thumbs-down and it would probably have remained a little-known misadventure of cinematic history had it not been re-released to cash in on the Tolkien-boom derived from the three-film series by Peter Jackson. Warner Studios released a sequel *The Return of the King* to complete the animated version of the tale. An animated film of *The Hobbit* was released in 1977, also by Warner.

Jackson's cinematic treatment is in the big-budget action adventure style of film-making. The decision to shoot the story as three films (corresponding fairly closely to the three volumes of the original *The Lord of the Rings* publication) has allowed the director and his associates the time and opportunity to develop lavish effects without neglecting characterisation and sub-plot. Jackson's team evidently put a lot of love and care into getting it 'right', as far as taking snippets of dialogue and re-using them elsewhere and in other contexts than the original, in order not to have to drop in invented dialogue for the characters. Naturally, this decision has not been universally approved.

There has of course been criticism: mainly that (i) the films are too long, (ii) the films are too short, (iii) there have been too few concessions to the cinematic medium, and that (iv) there have been too many. In short, those who will not accept any version of *The Lord of the Rings* not stemming directly from the master's pen have pronounced themselves bitterly disappointed with the project. Others, who would happily have consigned the whole affair – books, films, plays and all – to the rubbish bin of cultural history, have howled in protest at the seemingly never-ending onward march of Tolkien's work.

Much of the story is practically unfilmable and interpretations of all aspects will vary. No two people will have the same mental picture of an Ent or a Nazgûl. The film-maker is also constrained by the maxim "show, don't tell" which necessitates a strong visual quality to every action – often different from the action in the book.

On balance, the three-film set (available in cinematic and extended-play home-viewing versions) will certainly have introduced the story to people who would never contemplate reading over a thousand pages of text. There can be no valid reason for denying them the pleasure of enjoying Tolkien's sub-created world, albeit at second hand through the camera lens.

Perhaps the gravest charge that can be laid at the door of Jackson's films is the gratuitous exploitation of Tolkien's work. Fans and students can accept derivative maps, art prints, audio tapes and compact discs based on *The Lord of the Rings*, but many are less comfortable with Sauron as a 12" poseable action figure or novelty fridge magnet.

At the time of writing, there are plans for a further adventure set in Middle-Earth, concerning the search of Ancanar, a nobleman, for the Elven city.

Worldwide Appeal

What is the nature of the worldwide appeal of *The Lord of the Rings*? This is a difficult question to answer and it is fair to say that professional critics of literature have consistently shot themselves in the foot in their criticism of the work and their predictions for it.

At first publication, the books were in many respects a complete departure from canonical modern English literature. They were, for example, essentially works of fantasy and therefore aimed at what was then a marginal market. The story was very long at over 1000 pages of text, plus numerous appendices, at a time when the sprawling novel was no longer in vogue. They were also demanding books, with some sections in languages other than Modern English - languages moreover which no-one but the author knew. The whole project must have seemed like a publisher's and a reader's nightmare. Yet somehow it worked.

The early critics were generally rather sniffy, as they did not know what to make of the work. Some were outright hostile, others bemused; they took refuge in the familiar commonplaces of literary criticism and reproved the books for having no character development, indeed no real characters at all, in stock situations with which the reader could feel no sympathy, all written up in an absurd archaic, mock-heroic form of language. The books were dismissed as irrelevant and silly, and likely to be forgotten in no time.

Criticism did not stop there. In fact, as the awareness dawned that the books were neither trivial, nor lightweight, nor likely to be forgotten, a whole new series of critical weaponry was brought to bear on the author and his works. One line of attack was to suggest that Tolkien was an ivory-tower academic, and his output could only appeal to readers with a similar inward-focussed mentality. Another suggested that the whole thing was trivial and its readers retarded. (It is curious that one set of reviewers could think the readers too academic, and another set think them too stupid!) Another tactic was to decry the lack of female characters, and to regard the story as a "boys'-own adventure". There may perhaps be more truth in this approach, since there are numerically few female characters with an integral part in the story: Galadriel, Eowynn and Arwen are the most notable 'female leads', to which listing one might add Shelob and Rosie Cotton. Admittedly Arwen is to some extent shadowy - the object of Aragorn's desire, but never really shown as a character in the full glare of narrative limelight. The others are central to the parts of the story in which they appear though, with Galadriel providing valuable support in the crisis after the fall of Gandalf, and gifts which will play a role later in the story (Sam's rope, Frodo's phial of light, Merry's brooch). The story of Eowyn, wound round the lives of both Aragorn and Faramir, is a main plot in itself. Her desire for escape, for a purpose worthy of her great courage and noble lineage, works to involve her in a doomed, unrequited love (with Aragorn) and later in a relationship of genuine affection with Faramir. (This latter theme leads to the union of the houses of Rohan and Gondor - with a consequent diminution of Numenorean blood, Tolkien implies. The higher races of Men are becoming more like the middle ones.)

Every new generation of critics has assailed the work with the fashionable objections of its day. None of them seem to have had any effect on sales and the popularity of the story. The hunger for hobbit-lore has spawned spin-offs – films, diaries, maps and other treatments – and imitations. The latter are of variable quality, but even the most avid fantasy fan would admit that the literary merit of even the best is far short of the original work. It is of course a lot easier to find your way when someone has already trodden the path before you.

(In fairness, Tolkien was not the first writer of fantasy. In 1922 E.R. Eddison published *The Worm Ourobouros*, a tale set on another planet but with a basis in European folklore. Tolkien admired the tale, but felt he could make a better one, more firmly rooted in the soil of Middle-Earth. There were also series of books about 'heroic' characters such as Conan around at this time.)

ɛ

The story is a global best-seller and has been translated into many other languages. That, in itself, does not mean a great deal since many pulp-fiction 'bestsellers' have received similar treatment. Most are sensationalised for a few months, and are soon forgotten when the next 'hot property' comes along. A few writers manage to stay at the top of the tree for years, producing series of books which sell countless copies. Many constantly re-write the same few tales – knowing that there is a market for such material, they are encouraged to stick with what sells. Tolkien cannot be criticised on that basis. While one might accuse the publisher of exploiting the Tolkien name for all it is worth, with a stream of earlier versions of the tales published in *The Lord of the Rings* and *The Silmarillion*, in fact there seems to be a genuine interest in, and appetite for, the formative stages in the matter of Middle-Earth. The public, it seems, cannot get enough of it.

The world-wide nature of the appeal of *The Lord of the Rings* can be seen in the various translations of the book. All major European languages have their own *The Lord of the Rings* now, and many of them can boast other works such as *The Hobbit* and *The Silmarillion*.

The principal problem in producing such translations is the use Tolkien made of archaic English. It is not just a few 'hither's, 'thou's and 'yon's sprinkled through the narrative, as in so many fantasy writers' output, but in many cases a fundamental indication of character - compare the formal speech of Elrond with the casual chattiness of the hobbits. Only Gandalf, and to a lesser extent Aragorn, manage to move from conversational to epic style and back again with ease.

There are even books available from one company (Walking Tree Publishers) offering guidance to translators: how to capture the archaic style in Norwegian, how to retain the reflection of character in Spanish, comparisons of translations into French, German, Dutch, Russian, Hebrew and even Esperanto[1]. One academic has formulated a theoretical model for handling the process and assessing the results. A series of essays deals with the reception of *The Lord of the Rings* in places such as India where the cultural assumptions can be very different from those in the Anglophone and European worlds

When the mere act of translation of a single author's output is enough to inspire a range of separate studies, then we are clearly dealing with a unique

---

[1] Website (http://privatewww.essex.ac.uk/~alan/tolkien/translations.html) lists the following languages for translations of some or all Tolkien's works: Armenian, Basque, Breton, Bulgarian, Byelorussian, Catalan, Chinese (Complex and Simple), Croatian, Czech, Danish, Dutch, Esperanto, Estonian, Faroese, Finnish, French, Galacian, German, Greek, Hebrew, Hungarian, Icelandic, Indonesian, Italian, Japanese, Korean, Latvian, Lithuanian, Luxembourgish, Marathi, Moldavian, Norwegian, Polish, Portuguese (European and Brazilian), Romanian, Russian, Serbian, Slovak, Slovenian, Spanish, Swedish, Thai, Turkish, Ukrainian. Depending on how one counts the variants (is Brazilian Portuguese a dialect of European Portuguese or a separate language?) this makes nearly fifty different translations of the English original.

Some language-study groups have had fun attempting translations of parts of the works into their respective target languages. These include Middle English, Old English, Latin, Quenya and Sindarin.

Tolkien societies sometimes use a word drawn from Elvish (e.g. Amon Hen) in their literature, while others opt for a direct translated term (e.g. the Italian *la Terra di Mezzo* 'the land of the Middle', Middle-Earth).

text requiring very careful handling. Needless to say, the act of translating the books into another language is to some extent like the act of turning them into radio plays or films: there is a trade-off between, on the one hand, authenticity and an accurate portrayal of the original and, on the other hand, producing something that will convey meaning to the intended audience. Translations can stick closely to the original or be quite liberal with it: the decision is the translator's and his work stands or falls by the effect on his audience.

There is a major pitfall in any attempt at wholesale translation: the relationship between the speech of Rohan and Westron is conveyed in the book by the skilful use of forms of Old English. (The language is not itself Old English as such, but rather a mix of ancient and modern, still intelligible to a reader of Modern English but heavily charged with ancient patterns of speech and thought.) In translating the work into, for example, Modern French, the faithful translator should try to use forms of the language which are heavily laden with terms and constructions from Old French; for German, the effect should be achieved with Old High German (Alamannic or Franconian), for Polish with Old Church Slavonic and so on. However, few (if any) translators choose to go this route wholeheartedly, partly because the effect has to be very finely judged by someone with a delicate ear for the language (another Tolkien, in fact) and partly because reproducing a harmonious and memorable name, such as Theoden, with an elegant word meaning 'lord of the free folk' (that is approximately what OE *þęoden* means) is often not possible in other cultures. Translators therefore generally retain character-names from the English text, and the effect on their readership is difficult to judge. (To a historically-minded speaker of Dutch, German, Norwegian, Swedish or Danish the name Theoden might conceivably conjure up a similar effect to the one Tolkien intended in English. Yet it is doubtful that many readers of the books know enough about Anglo-Saxon England to make any connection at all between the name Theoden and the office of 'folk-leader' in England before the Norman invasion.) Likewise, the names Balin and Durin occur in mediaeval literature ('English Arthurian' and 'Icelandic mythological' respectively) and are usually left in their English forms (e.g. French "la tombe de Balin", "la porte de Durin"). This approach saves translators a good deal of time and trouble, and furthermore can be defended in terms of faithfulness to the English original.

Quite what the appeal of Tolkien's work is to non-Anglophones is difficult to assess, lacking the resonances of historical matter that the names and language convey in the original. The notion of a world similar to our own but governed by rather different physical and moral laws is no doubt part of it. Prophecy can have a direct effect, for example – most major characters have an adage or two at hand to underline their expectations, such as 'oft evil will shall evil mar'. The struggle of 'good' with 'evil' is played out in various formats (from alien invasions to the Wild West) but usually without any pretence to literary merit. Perhaps it lies, in the end, in the very satisfying quality which Tolkien himself called 'sub-creation' – the process of creating an artificial world which the mind of the reader can enter and explore. This quality is abundant in Tolkien's work, and present to greater or lesser extent in the works of many other fiction writers. The pace of the tale – here I mean *The Lord of the Rings* – is carefully judged to lure the reader in, then gradually drag him along in a tempest of action and finally slacken slowly back to the rather languid pace of the opening chapter by the close. No wonder readers who have finished the story are often moved to start at the beginning again without a break. This inclusiveness, this feeling that the reader somehow 'belongs' in the sub-created world and the wish to explore it all over again, may account for the fierce loyalty Tolkien enjoys as a writer – and for the equally fierce loathing (whether disguised as literary criticism or political opprobrium) he inspires in others.

Rollo May, the noted psychoanalyst, wrote: "A myth is a way of making sense in a senseless world. .... Myths give us relief from neurotic guilt and excessive anxiety. They are self-interpretations of our inner selves in relation to the outside world. The person without a myth is a person without a home."

This insight into the nature of the mythic narrative perhaps explains some of the fierce adherence to Tolkien's works. The great quest undertaken by a small, frightened but determined individual resonates with modern people who feel every bit as small and frightened, but also lost and lonely in a meaningless existence. They lack a meaningful 'myth', a structuring principle in their lives (having long ago abandoned the contradictory dogma of formal religion, and more recently having become disillusioned with the idealistic notions of progress and science) and they find that *The Lord of the Rings* fulfils that role. Whether they *like* Frodo, or Gandalf, or Saruman is not important. The fact that – within the tale – these characters have meaningful lives is at the root of the story's profound appeal. They each have a real responsibility, have a direct effect on their communities, and in the end they *mean* something.

Allied to this deep mythic sense is the nostalgia many English people feel for the 'green and pleasant land' they grew up in, no matter how besmirched it may have been with tarmac and concrete. Enough remains of rural England to show how beautiful and welcoming it must once have been – and it is in the nature of the nostalgic to imagine the past as fundamentally better than the present.

According to one interpretation of skeletal evidence, the average height of adults in the early Anglo-Saxon period was greater than at any subsequent time in English history down to the latter half of the 20th century. The early Anglo-Saxons had a better, more nutritious and varied diet than in subsequent periods – probably because their total numbers were below two million during this time and contemporary agriculture could support that level of population. They enjoyed the benefits of small political units, which kept leaders responsive to the needs of their folk, and of many small religious and social centres. Tolkien probably drew on Anglo-Saxon institutions[1] for the hobbits

---

[1] The relatively small-scale nature of Anglo-Saxon political and strategic thinking was a factor in the Danish invasions: kingdoms were picked off one-by-one by a determined and well-organised foe. The England that emerged from the first Danish Wars under King Alfred the

and Rohirrim, partly because they were natural to the English, and partly because they represent a very comfortable level of achievement matching available resources to the needs of the community.

Tolkien's Middle-Earth is also a world in which the competing demands of nature and civilisation are balanced. The hobbits live a rustic life of (relative) peace and (relative) plenty, and they have no complex machines or industrial processes. While the drudgery of rural agricultural work must often have been no less gruelling than factory-work today, there is a certain appeal to the outdoor life in agreeable surroundings complemented by big meals and strong drink. This also appeals to many modern people, living in western societies where industrialisation has often given way to urban decay and the destruction of social systems through immense upheavals in communities.

A yearning for meaning in our lives is part of the religious impulse, a basic human need to be part of something worthwhile. For those whose lives are often dull, repetitive or simply aimless, Tolkien's morally-directed world feels more like home than the real world.

Great and his heirs had learnt the lesson well, and achieved a level of political cohesion unique in Europe at that time.

Appendix 1 - Timeline

The characters and events in the narrative are closely woven together, and the narrative often drops one thread to pick up another, so that it can be very difficult to ascertain the chronology of events.

The following is an attempt to show the sequence of meetings and partings as an aid to understanding the text.

Note: February has 30 days in the Shire calendar.

Shire Year 3018		
April	12	Gandalf returns to Hobbiton with news for Frodo that he suspects Bilbo's Ring to be the One Ring
May		-
June (late in the month)		Gandalf leaves Hobbiton to consult Saruman
July	4	Boromir leaves Minas Tirith for Rivendell to seek the meaning of his dreams
	10	Gandalf rejects Saruman's offer to join him; Saruman imprisons him in Isengard
August		Gollum enters Moria
September	18	Gandalf is rescued from Orthanc by Gwaihir
	19	Gandalf reaches Edoras
	21	Gandalf chooses Shadowfax
	22	Frodo celebrates his birthday with his friends
September	23	Fatty and Merry leave for Crickhollow early, followed by Pippin, Sam and Frodo in the evening; Gandalf sets off for Hobbiton
	25	Frodo's party reaches Crickhollow
	26	The four hobbits are captured by Old Man Willow, rescued by Tom Bombadil, stay with Tom overnight
	28	Hobbits leave Tom, are captured by the Barrow-wights and rescued by Tom

	29	Gandalf reaches Hobbiton, learns of Frodo's departure from the Gaffer; Hobbits arrive at Bree, spend the night at the inn, meet Strider
	30	Black Riders raid the inn at Bree; Hobbits and Strider leave Bree; Gandalf arrives at Bree too late, misses them
October	1	Gandalf leaves Bree in search of the hobbits
	3	Gandalf reaches Weathertop, is attacked by Nazgûl
	6	Hobbits reach Weathertop; Frodo is wounded in a night attack by Nazgûl
	9	Glorfindel leaves Rivendell in search of Gandalf
	13	Hobbits reach Bridge of Mitheithel
	18	Gandalf reaches Rivendell; Glorfindel finds Frodo on the road
	20	Frodo escapes pursuit at Ford of Bruinen with Glorfindel's help
	24	Boromir arrives in Rivendell; Frodo wakes up in Rivendell, is re-united with the other hobbits and Gandalf
	25	Council of Elrond is held in Rivendell
November		-
December	25	Fellowship of the Ring leaves Rivendell,
Shire Year 3019		
January	11	Fellowship attempts to cross the Misty Mountains over the pass of Caradhras and is beaten back
	13	Fellowship reaches the West Gate of Moria, pursued by Gollum
	15	Gandalf falls fighting the Balrog; rest of the Fellowship flees
	16	Fellowship arrives in Lothlorien
	17	Fellowship is conducted to Caras Galadhon
	23	Gandalf and the Balrog fight on Zirakzigil
	25	Gandalf overcomes the Balrog, and passes out of the world
February	14	Gandalf returns to Middle-Earth; Frodo looks into the Mirror of Galadriel

	16	Fellowship leaves Lothlorien
	17	Gandalf is deposited in Lothlorien by Gwaihir
	23	Fellowship is attacked at Sarn Gebir
	25	Fellowship passes the Argonath and camps at Parth Galen; Theoden's son, Theodred is slain at the Ford of Isen
	26	Boromir attempts to seize the Ring; the Fellowship is broken; Orcs seize Merry and Pippin, kill Boromir; Frodo and Sam escape across the River Anduin to the Emyn Muil; Aragorn, Legolas and Gimli arrange Boromir's funeral then begin to pursue the Orcs
	29	Orcs attacked by Rohirrim, Merry and Pippin escape, meet Treebeard; Frodo and Sam capture Gollum, who agrees to guide them to the Black Gate; Faramir sees Boromir's body float past on the Anduin
	30	Treebeard holds the Entmoot
March	1	Aragorn, Gimli & Legolas met Gandalf the White in Fangorn Forest; Gollum leads Frodo and Sam across the Dead Marshes
	2	Aragorn, Gimli, Legolas and Gandalf reach Edoras and heal King Theoden; the Ents march to Isengard
	3	Ents tear down Isengard, imprison Saruman and Grima in Orthanc; battle of Helm's Deep; Frodo, Sam and Gollum reach the edge of the Morannon wasteland; Gandalf and Theoden leave for Isengard
	5	Theoden, Aragorn, Legolas and Gimli meet Pippin and Merry at Isengard; Saruman's parley and Grima's attack with the palantir; Gandalf and Pippin ride off for Minas Tirith
	6	Theoden and Merry leave for Harrowdale; the Dunedain arrive with news for Aragorn
	7	Faramir captures Frodo and Sam, takes them to Henneth Annun
	8	Frodo, Sam and Gollum leave Henneth Annun for Cirith Ungol; Aragorn, Gimli and Legolas set out on the Paths of the Dead with the Dunedain

	9	Aragorn's group reach the Stone of Erech and invoke the oath of the Dead; Thedoen and Merry reach Dunharrow; Gandalf and Pippin reach Minas Tirith; Frodo's group reach the Morgul road
March	10	Muster of Rohan; Rohirrim leave Harrowdale with Merry and Eowyn; Gandalf challenges the Nazgûl at the Great Gate, saves Faramir; Frodo's group see the Nazgûl's army leave Minas Morgul
	12	Gollum leads Frodo and Sam into Shelob's lair; Aragorn's group drives back the enemy at Pelargir; Theoden's army camps at Minrimmon
	13	Aragorn's group captures the black fleet; Rohirrim enter Druadan Forest; Faramir is wounded in Osgilliath; Frodo is captured by the Orcs from Cirith Ungol
	14	Sam enters Cirith Ungol in search of Frodo; Mordor's army reaches Minas Tirith and lays seige to the city; Rohirrim reach the Grey Wood
	15	Sam and Frodo escape from Cirith Ungol, begin the journey north; Battle of Pelennor Fields; the Nazgûl breaks the Great Gate and is slain in the fighting; Theoden dies in battle; Aragorn raises his royal standard before the city
	16	Commanders of the West hold a counsel of war; Denethor takes his own life;
	18	The Great Host of the west sets out for Mordor; Faramir, Merry and Eowyn remain behind in Minas Tirith; Frodo and Sam are captured by Orcs
	19	The Host reaches Morgul Vale; Frodo and Sam escape and head for Barad-dûr
	22	Frodo and Sam head for Mount Doom
	23	The Host leaves Ithilien; Frodo and Sam leave behind their weapons and supplies
	24	The Host reaches the Morannon; Frodo and Sam reach the foot of Mount Doom
	25	The Host is surrounded and gives battle; Frodo and Sam reach the Cracks of Doom, Gollum attempts to snatch the Ring; the Ring is destroyed, the Dark Tower falls.
April		

May	1	Aragorn is crowned King Elessar; Elrond and Arwen set out from Rivendell
	20	Elrond and Arwen reach Lothlorien
June	16	Elrond and Arwen set out for Minas Tirith
July	1	Arwen arrives in Minas Tirith, marries King Elessar
	19	Theoden's funeral party leaves for Edoras
August	10	Theoden's funeral; Eomer returns to Rohan as king
	14	Funeral guests leave Rohan
	22	Guests arrive at Isengard, the Fellowship is formally dissolved
	28	Returning hobbits overtake Saruman and Grima on the road north
September	22	Fellowship celebrates Bilbo's 129th birthday in Rivendell; Saruman arrives in the Shire
October	5	Gandalf and the hobbits leave Rivendell for the Shire
	30	Hobbits reach the Shire; Gandalf reaches Bombadil's house
November	3	Battle of Bywater, Saruman defeated; Grima kills Saruman

Bibliography

Note - The works of Tolkien himself are not cited here.

ALLEN, J. (ED.) *An Introduction to Elvish*, Glenfinnan, 1978 (reprinted 2001)

- *Quenya Grammar and Dictionary* in Allen, 1978
- *Sindarin Grammar and Dictionary* in Allen, 1978
- *Proto-Eldarin Consonants* in Allen, 1978
- *Other Tongues* in Allen, 1978
- *The Evolution of the Tengwar* in Allen, 1978
- *The Runes* in Allen, 1978

BATES, B. *The Real Middle Earth*, London, 2002

BRANSTON, B. *The Lost Gods of England,* London, 1974

- *Gods of the North*, London, 1980

BRUCE-MITFORD, R. *The Sutton Hoo Ship Burial* Vol.3 (parts 1 & 2) London 1983

CARPENTER, H. *The Letters of J.R.R.Tolkien*, Boston, 2000

CHANCE, J. *Tolkien's Art*, Lexington, 2001

CLARK-HALL, J.R. *A Concise Anglo-Saxon Dictionary*, Toronto, 1984

CURRY, P. *Defending Middle-Earth – Tolkien, Myth and Modernity*, London, 1997

DAY, D. *The Tolkien Companion*, London, 1993

GARMONSWAY, G.N. *An Early Norse Reader*, Cambridge, 1928

GILSON, C. & WELDEN, B. *Proto-Eldarin Vowels: A Comparative Survey* in Allen, 1978

KRIEG, L.J. *The Tengwar of Feanor* in Allen, 1978

- *A Survey of Some English-Tengwar Orthographies* in Allen, 1978

MAY, R. *The Cry for Myth*, London, 1993

MENN, L. *Elvish Loanwords in Indo-European: Cultural Implications* in Allen, 1978

NOEL, R.S. *The Mythology of Middle-earth*, London, 1977

- *The Languages of Tolkien's Middle-Earth*, Boston, 1980

North, R. *Heathen Gods in Old English Literature, Cambridge, 1997*

Oosten, J.G *The War of the Gods. The Social Code in Indo-European Mythology*, London, 1985

Pollington, S *Leechcraft - Early English Charms, Plantlore and Healing*, Hockwold-cum-Wilton, 2000

- *The English Warrior from Earliest Times to 1066*, Hockwold-cum-Wilton, 2001

Puhvel, J. *Comparative Mythology*, Baltimore, 1987

Rives, J.B. (Trans.) *Tacitus - Germania,* Oxford, 1999

Scott Littleton, C. *The New Comparative Mythology. An Anthropological Assessment of the Theories of Georges Dumezil*, London, 1973

Shippey, T. *J.R.R.Tolkien – Author of the Century*, New York, 2002

- *Old English Verse*, London, 1972

Stone, A. *Ymir's Flesh: Northern European Creation Mythologies,* Loughborough, 1997

Wallace-Hadrill, J.M. *Early Germanic Kingship in England and on the Continent*, Oxford, 1971

Wrenn, C.L. *Beowulf with the Finnsburg Fragment*, London, 1973

Some of our other titles

The English Warrior from earliest times to 1066

Stephen Pollington

This is not intended to be a bald listing of the battles and campaigns from the Anglo-Saxon Chronicle and other sources, but rather it is an attempt to get below the surface of Anglo-Saxon warriorhood and to investigate the rites, social attitudes, mentality and mythology of the warfare of those times.

> "An under-the-skin study of the role, rights, duties, psyche and rituals of the Anglo-Saxon warrior. The author combines original translations from Norse and Old English primary sources with archaeological and linguistic evidence for an in-depth look at the warrior, his weapons, tactics and logistics.
>
> A very refreshing, innovative and well-written piece of scholarship that illuminates a neglected period of English history"
>
> *Time Team Booklists* - Channel 4 Television

Revised Edition

An already highly acclaimed book has been made even better by the inclusion of additional information and illustrations.

£14.95 ISBN 1–898281–27–0 9½" x 6¾"/245 x 170mm over 50 illustrations 288 pages

The Mead Hall The feasting tradition in Anglo-Saxon England

Stephen Pollington

This new study takes a broad look at the subject of halls and feasting in Anglo-Saxon England. The idea of the communal meal was very important among nobles and yeomen, warriors, farmers churchmen and laity. One of the aims of the book is to show that there was not just one 'feast' but two main types: the informal social occasion *gebeorscipe* and the formal, ritual gathering *symbel.*

Using the evidence of Old English texts - mainly the epic *Beowulf* and the *Anglo-Saxon Chronicles*, Stephen Pollington shows that the idea of feasting remained central to early English social traditions long after the physical reality had declined in importance.

The words of the poets and saga-writers are supported by a wealth of archaeological data dealing with halls, settlement layouts and magnificent feasting gear found in many early Anglo-Saxon graves.

Three appendices cover:

Hall-themes in Old English verse;

Old English and translated texts;

The structure and origins of the warband.

£14.95 ISBN 1-898281-30-0 9 ¾ x 6 ¾ inches 248 x 170mm 288 pages hardback

The Rebirth of England and English: The Vision of William Barnes

Fr. Andrew Phillips

English history is patterned with spirits so bright that they broke through convention and saw another England. Such was the case of the Dorset poet, William Barnes (1801–86), priest, poet, teacher, self-taught polymath, linguist extraordinary and that rare thing – a man of vision. In this work the author looks at that vision, a vision at once of Religion, Nature, Art, Marriage, Society, Economics, Politics and Language. He writes: 'In search of authentic English roots and values, our post-industrial society may well have much to learn from Barnes'.

£4.95 A5 ISBN 1–898281–17–3 160pp

Monasteriales Indicia

The Anglo-Saxon Monastic Sign Language

Edited with notes and translation by Debby Banham

The *Monasteriales Indicia* is one of very few texts which let us see how evryday life was lived in monasteries in the early Middle Ages. Written in Old English and preserved in a manuscript of the mid-eleventh century, it consists of 127 signs used by Anglo-Saxon monks during the times when the Benedictine Rule forbade them to speak. These indicate the foods the monks ate, the clothes they wore, and the books they used in church and chapter, as well as the tools they used in their daily life, and persons they might meet both in the monastery and outside. The text is printed here with a parallel translation. The introduction gives a summary of the background, both historical and textual, as well as a brief look at the later evidence for monastic sign language in England.

£4.95 A5 ISBN 0–9516209–4–0 96pp

The Battle of Maldon: Text and Translation

Translated and edited by Bill Griffiths

The Battle of Maldon was fought between the men of Essex and the Vikings in AD 991. The action was captured in an Anglo-Saxon poem whose vividness and heroic spirit has fascinated readers and scholars for generations. *The Battle of Maldon* includes the source text; edited text; parallel literal translation; verse translation; a review of 103 books and articles.

This edition has a helpful guide to Old English verse.

£4.95 A5 ISBN 0–9516209–0–8 96pp

Beowulf: Text and Translation

Translated by John Porter

The verse in which the story unfolds is, by common consent, the finest writing surviving in Old English, a text that all students of the language and many general readers will want to tackle in the original form. To aid understanding of the Old English, a literal word-by-word translation is printed opposite the edited text and provides a practical key to this Anglo-Saxon masterpiece.

£8.95 A5 ISBN 0–9516209–2–4 192pp

An Introduction to Early English Law

Bill Griffiths

Much of Anglo-Saxon life followed a traditional pattern, of custom, and of dependence on kin-groups for land, support and security. The Viking incursions of the ninth century and the reconquest of the north that followed both disturbed this pattern and led to a new emphasis on centralized power and law, with royal and ecclesiastical officials prominent as arbitrators and settlers of disputes. The diversity and development of early English law is sampled here by selecting several law-codes to be read in translation - that of Æthelbert of Kent, being the first to be issued in England, Alfred the Great's, the most clearly thought-out of all, and short codes from the reigns of Edmund and Æthelred the Unready.

£4.95 A5 ISBN 1–898281–14–9 96pp

The Hallowing of England

A Guide to the Saints of Old England and their Places of Pilgrimage

Fr. Andrew Philips

In the Old English period we can count over 300 saints, yet today their names and exploits are largely unknown. They are part of a forgotten England which, though it lies deep in the past, is an important part of our national and spiritual history. This guide includes a list of saints, an alphabetical list of places with which they are associated, and a calendar of saint's feast days.

£4.95 A5 ISBN 1–898281–08–4 96pp

Alfred's Metres of Boethius

edited by Bill Griffiths

In this new edition of the Old English *Metres of Boethius*, clarity of text, informative notes and a helpful glossary have been a priority, for this is one of the most approachable of Old English verse texts. Its clear, expositional verse style makes it an ideal starting point for all amateurs of the period.

In these poems, King Alfred re-built the Latin verses from Boethius' *De Consolatione Philosophiae* ("On the Consolation of Philosophy") into new alliterative poems, via an Old English prose intermediary. The stirring images and stories of Boethius' original are retained - streams, legends, animals, volcanoes - and developed for an Anglo-Saxon audience to include the Gothic invasion of Italy (Metre 1), the figure of Welland the Smith (Metre 10), and the hugely disconcerting image of Death's hunt for mankind (Metre 27). The text is in effect a compendium of late classical science and philosophy, tackling serious issues like the working of the universe, the nature of the soul, the morality of power - but presented in so clear and lively a manner as to make it as challenging today as it was in those surprisingly UN-Dark Ages.

The text is in Old English without Modern English translation

£14.95 10" x 7" (250 x 175mm) ISBN 1–898281–03–1 208pp

A Handbook of Anglo-Saxon Food: Processing and Consumption

Ann Hagen

For the first time information from various sources has been brought together in order to build up a picture of how food was grown, conserved, prepared and eaten during the period from the beginning of the 5th century to the 11th century. Many people will find it fascinating for the views it gives of an important aspect of Anglo-Saxon life and culture. In addition to Anglo-Saxon England the Celtic west of Britain is also covered. Now with an extensive index.

£9.95 A5 ISBN 0–9516209–8–3 192pp

A Second Handbook of Anglo-Saxon Food & Drink

Production and Distribution

Ann Hagen

Food production for home consumption was the basis of economic activity throughout the Anglo-Saxon period. This second handbook complements the first and brings together a vast amount of information on livestock, cereal and vegetable crops, fish, honey and fermented drinks. Related subjects such as hospitality, charity and drunkenness are also dealt with. Extensive index.

£14.95 A5 ISBN 1–898281–12–2 432pp

English Heroic Legends

Kathleen Herbert

The author has taken the skeletons of ancient Germanic legends about great kings, queens and heroes, and put flesh on them. Kathleen Herbert's extensive knowledge of the period is reflected in the wealth of detail she brings to these tales of adventure, passion, bloodshed and magic.

The book is in two parts. First are the stories that originate deep in the past, yet because they have not been hackneyed, they are still strange and enchanting. After that there is a selection of the source material, with information about where it can be found and some discussion about how it can be used.

£9-95 A5 ISBN 0–9516209–9–1 292pp

Peace-Weavers and Shield-Maidens: Women in Early English Society

Kathleen Herbert

The recorded history of the English people did not start in 1066 as popularly believed but one-thousand years earlier. The Roman historian Cornelius Tacitus noted in *Germania*, published in the year 98, that the English (Latin *Anglii*), who lived in the southern part of the Jutland peninsula, were members of an alliance of Goddess-worshippers. The author has taken that as an appropriate opening to an account of the earliest Englishwomen, the part they played in the making of England, what they did in peace and war, the impressions they left in Britain and on the continent, how they were recorded in the chronicles, how they come alive in heroic verse and riddles.

£4.95 A5 ISBN 1–898281–11–4 64pp

Anglo-Saxon Runes

John. M. Kemble

Kemble's essay *On Anglo-Saxon Runes* first appeared in the journal *Archaeologia* for 1840; it draws on the work of Wilhelm Grimm, but breaks new ground for Anglo-Saxon studies in his survey of the Ruthwell Cross and the Cynewulf poems. It is an expression both of his own indomitable spirit and of the fascination and mystery of the Runes themselves, making one of the most attractive introductions to the topic. For this edition new notes have been supplied, which include translations of Latin and Old English material quoted in the text, to make this key work in the study of runes more accessible to the general reader.

£4.95 A5 ISBN 0–9516209–1–6 80pp

Looking for the Lost Gods of England

Kathleen Herbert

Kathleen Herbert sifts through the royal genealogies, charms, verse and other sources to find clues to the names and attributes of the Gods and Goddesses of the early English. The earliest account of English heathen practices reveals that they worshipped the Earth Mother and called her Nerthus. The tales, beliefs and traditions of that time are still with us in, for example, Sand able to stir our minds and imaginations.

£4.95 A5 ISBN 1–898281–04–1 64pp

Rudiments of Runelore

Stephen Pollington

This book provides both a comprehensive introduction for those coming to the subject for the first time, and a handy and inexpensive reference work for those with some knowledge of the subject. The *Abecedarium Nordmannicum* and the English, Norwegian and Icelandic rune poems are included in their original and translated form. Also included is work on the three Brandon runic inscriptions and the Norfolk 'Tiw' runes.

£4.95 A5 ISBN 1–898281–16–5 Illustrations 88pp

Rune Cards

Tony Linsell and Brian Partridge

> "This boxed set of 30 cards contains some of the most beautiful and descriptive black and white line drawings that I have ever seen on this subject."
>
> ***Pagan News***

30 pen and ink drawings by Brian Partridge

80 page booklet by Tony Linsell gives information about the origin of runes, their meaning, and how to read them.

£9.95 ISBN 1-898281-34-3 30 cards 85mm x 132mm - boxed with booklet

Dark Age Naval Power

A Reassessment of Frankish and Anglo-Saxon Seafaring Activity

John Haywood

In the first edition of this work, published in 1991, John Haywood argued that the capabilities of the pre-Viking Germanic seafarers had been greatly underestimated. Since that time, his reassessment of Frankish and Anglo-Saxon shipbuilding and seafaring has been widely praised and accepted.

In this second edition, some sections of the book have been revised and updated to include information gained from excavations and sea trials with sailing replicas of early ships. The new evidence supports the author's argument that early Germanic shipbuilding and seafaring skills were far more advanced than previously thought. It also supports the view that Viking ships and seaborne activities were not as revolutionary as is commonly believed.

> 'The book remains a historical study of the first order. It is required reading for our seminar on medieval seafaring at Texas A & M University and is essential reading for anyone interested in the subject.'
>
> F. H. Van Doorninck, *The American Neptune*

UK £14.95 ISBN 1-898281-22-X approx. 10 x 6½ inches - 245 x 170 mm 224 pages

English Martial Arts

Terry Brown

Little is known about the very early history of English martial arts but it is likely that methods, techniques and principles were passed on from one generation to the next for centuries. By the sixteenth century English martial artists had their own governing body which controlled its members in much the same way as do modern-day martial arts organisations. It is apparent from contemporary evidence that the Company of Maisters taught and practised a fighting system that ranks as high in terms of effectiveness and pedigree as any in the world.

In the first part of the book the author investigates the weapons, history and development of the English fighting system and looks at some of the attitudes, beliefs and social pressures that helped mould it.

Part two deals with English fighting techniques drawn from books and manuscripts that recorded the system at various stages in its history. In other words, all of the methods and techniques shown in this book are authentic and have not been created by the author. The theories that underlie the system are explained in a chapter on *The Principles of True Fighting.* All of the techniques covered are illustrated with photographs and accompanied by instructions. Techniques included are for bare-fist fighting, broadsword, quarterstaff, bill, sword and buckler, sword and dagger.

Experienced martial artists, irrespective of the style they practice, will recognise that the techniques and methods of this system are based on principles that are as valid as those underlying the system that they practice.

The author, who has been a martial artist for twenty-eight years, has recently re-formed the Company of Maisters of Defence, a medieval English martial arts organization.

£16.95 ISBN 1–898281–29-7 10 x 6½ inches - 245 x 170 mm 220 photographs 240 pages

A Guide to Late Anglo-Saxon England

From Alfred to Eadgar II 871–1074

Donald Henson

This guide has been prepared with the aim of providing the general readers with both an overview of the period and a wealth of background information. Facts and figures are presented in a way that makes this a useful reference handbook.

Contents include: The Origins of England; Physical Geography; Human Geography; English Society; Government and Politics; The Church; Language and Literature; Personal Names; Effects of the Norman Conquest. All of the kings from Alfred to Eadgar II are dealt with separately and there is a chronicle of events for each of their reigns. There are also maps, family trees and extensive appendices.

£9.95 ISBN 1–898281–21–1 9½" x 6¾"/245 x 170mm, 6 maps & 3 family trees 208 pages

The English Elite in 1066 - Gone but not forgotten

Donald Henson

The people listed in this book formed the topmost section of the ruling elite in 1066. It includes all those who held office between the death of Eadward III (January 1066) and the abdication of Eadgar II (December 1066). There are 455 individuals in the main entries and these have been divided according to their office or position.

The following information is listed where available:

- What is known of their life;
- Their landed wealth;
- The early sources in which information about the individual can be found
- Modern references that give details about his or her life.

In addition to the biographical details, there is a wealth of background information about English society and government. A series of appendices provide detailed information about particular topics or groups of people.

£16.95 ISBN 1–898281–26–2 250 x 175mm / 10 x 7 inches paperback 272 pages

Tastes of Anglo-Saxon England

Mary Savelli

These easy to follow recipes will enable you to enjoy a mix of ingredients and flavours that were widely known in Anglo-Saxon England but are rarely experienced today. In addition to the 46 recipes, there is background information about households and cooking techniques.

£4.95 ISBN 1-898281-28-9 A5 80 pages

First Steps in Old English

An easy to follow language course for the beginner

Stephen Pollington

A complete, well presented and easy to use Old English language course which contains all the exercises and texts needed to learn Old English. This course has been designed to be of help to a wide range of students, from those who are teaching themselves at home, to undergraduates who are learning Old English as part of their English degree course. The author is aware that some individuals have little aptitude for learning languages and that many have difficulty with grammar. To help overcome these problems he has adopted a step by step approach that enables students of differing abilities to advance at their own pace. The course includes practice exercises.

£16.95 ISBN 1–898281–19–X 245mm x 170mm/10" x 6½" 240 pages

Ærgeweorc Old English Verse and Prose

read by Stephen Pollington

This audiotape cassette can be used with *First Steps in Old English* or just listened to for the sheer pleasure of hearing Old English spoken well.

Tracks: 1. Deor. 2. Beowulf – The Funeral of Scyld Scefing. 3. Engla Tocyme (The Arrival of the English). 4. Ines Domas. Two Extracts from the Laws of King Ine. 5. Deniga Hergung (The Danes' Harrying) Anglo-Saxon Chronicle Entry AD997. 6. Durham 7. The Ordeal (Be ðon ðe ordales weddigaþ) 8. Wið Dweorh (Against a Dwarf) 9. Wið Wennum (Against Wens) 10. Wið Wæterælfadle (Against Waterelf Sickness) 11. The Nine Herbs Charm 12. Læcedomas (Leechdoms) 13. Beowulf's Greeting 14. The Battle of Brunanburh 15. Blacmon – by Adrian Pilgrim.

£7.50 ISBN 1–898281–20–3 C40 audiotape

Wordcraft: Concise English/Old English Dictionary and Thesaurus

Stephen Pollington

This book provides Old English equivalents to the commoner modern words in both dictionary and thesaurus formats. The Thesaurus presents vocabulary relevant to a wide range of individual topics in alphabetical lists, thus making it easily accessible to those with specific areas of interest. Each thematic listing is encoded for cross-reference from the Dictionary. The two sections will be of invaluable assistance to students of the language, as well as to those with either a general or a specific interest in the Anglo-Saxon period.

£9.95 A5 ISBN 1–898281–02–5 256pp

An Introduction to the Old English Language and its Literature

Stephen Pollington

The purpose of this general introduction to Old English is not to deal with the teaching of Old English but to dispel some misconceptions about the language and to give an outline of its structure and its literature. Some basic knowledge of these is essential to an understanding of the early period of English history and the present form of the language.

£4.95 A5 ISBN 1–898281–06–8 48pp

Anglo-Saxon Riddles

Translated by John Porter

Here you will find ingenious characters who speak their names in riddles, and meet a one-eyed garlic seller, a bookworm, an iceberg, an oyster, the sun and moon and a host of others from the everyday life and imagination of the Anglo-Saxons. Their sense of the awesome power of creation goes hand in hand with a frank delight in obscenity, a fascination with disguise and with the mysterious processes by which the natural world is turned to human use. This edition contains **all 95 riddles of the Exeter Book in both Old English and Modern English.**

£4.95 A5 ISBN 1–898281–13–0 144pp

Anglo-Saxon Books

Frithgarth, Thetford Forest Park, Hockwold-cum-Wilton, Norfolk IP26 4NQ

Tel: 01842 828430 Fax: 01842 828332 email: enq@asbooks.co.uk

Further details of titles are available on our web site at www.asbooks.co.uk

Payment may be made by Visa / Mastercard or by a cheque drawn on a UK bank in sterling.

If you are paying by cheque please make it payable to Anglo-Saxon Books and enclose it with your order. When ordering by post please write clearly.

UK deliveries add 10% up to a maximum of £2· 50

Europe – including **Republic of Ireland** – add 10% plus £1 – all orders are sent airmail

North America add 10% surface delivery, 30% airmail

Elsewhere add 10% surface delivery, 40% airmail

Overseas surface delivery 6 – 10 weeks; airmail 6 – 14 days

Most titles are available in North America from bookstores.

Organisations

Þa Engliscan Gesiðas

Þa Engliscan Gesiðas (The English Companions) is a historical and cultural society exclusively devoted to Anglo-Saxon history. Its aims are to bridge the gap between scholars and non-experts, and to bring together all those with an interest in the Anglo-Saxon period, its language, culture and traditions, so as to promote a wider interest in, and knowledge of all things Anglo-Saxon. The Fellowship publishes a journal, *Wiðowinde,* which helps members to keep in touch with current thinking on topics from art and archaeology to heathenism and Early English Christianity. The Fellowship enables like-minded people to keep in contact by publicising conferences, courses and meetings which might be of interest to its members.

For further details see www.kami.demon.co.uk/gesithas/ or write to: The Membership Secretary, Þa Engliscan Gesiðas, BM Box 4336, London, WC1N 3XX England.

Regia Anglorum

Regia Anglorum was founded to accurately re-create the life of the British people as it was around the time of the Norman Conquest. Our work has a strong educational slant. We consider authenticity to be of prime importance and prefer, where possible, to work from archaeological materials. Approximately twenty-five per cent of our members, of over 500 people, are archaeologists or historians.

The Society has a large working Living History Exhibit, teaching and exhibiting more than twenty crafts in an authentic environment. We own a forty-foot wooden ship replica of a type that would have been a common sight in Northern European waters around the turn of the first millennium AD. Battle re-enactment is another aspect of our activities, often involving 200 or more warriors.

For further information see www.regia.org or contact: K. J. Siddorn, 9 Durleigh Close, Headley Park, Bristol BS13 7NQ, England, e-mail: kim_siddorn@compuserve.com

The Sutton Hoo Society

Our aims and objectives focus on promoting research and education relating to the Anglo Saxon Royal cemetery at Sutton Hoo, Suffolk in the UK. The Society publishes a newsletter SAXON twice a year, which keeps members up to date with society activities, carries resumes of lectures and visits, and reports progress on research and publication associated with the site. If you would like to join the Society please write to:

Membership Secretary, Sutton Hoo Society,
258 The Pastures, High Wycombe, Buckinghamshire HP13 5RS England
website: www.suttonhoo.org

Wuffing Education

Wuffing Education provides those interested in the history, archaeology, literature and culture of the Anglo-Saxons with the chance to meet experts and fellow enthusiasts for a whole day of in-depth seminars and discussions. Day Schools take place at the historic Tranmer House overlooking the burial mounds of Sutton Hoo in Suffolk.

For details of programme of events contact:-
Wuffing Education, 4 Hilly Fields, Woodbridge, Suffolk IP12 4DX
email education@wuffings.co.uk website www.wuffings.co.uk
Tel. 01394 383908 or 01728 688749

wyrd